# The Iceberg Agenda

## Mastering Corporate Potential

© Philip Atkinson 1998
First published 1998

Published by B T Batsford Ltd,
583 Fulham Road,
London SW6 5BY

Printed by
Redwood Books
Trowbridge
Wiltshire

ISBN 0 7134 8348 2

A CIP catalogue record for this book
is available from The British Library

# The Iceberg Agenda

Mastering Corporate
Potential

by

**Philip Atkinson**

B. T. BATSFORD LIMITED · LONDON

To
Ann, Sarah and Jonathan

# Contents

# Diagrams

# Tables

# Acknowledgements

There are so many people who have contributed towards my understanding and the practice of implementation of culture change that it is difficult to single out just a few. However, I would like to thank the following as well as those people who have attended my seminars and workshops over many years. It was through an exchange of views that I was able to gain a greater understanding of the dynamics that can shape our business for success. Thank you.

*Philip Atkinson*

David Buchanan, Brian Coolahan, David Deeble, Judith Dunker, John Ewart, Morris Foster, Keith Greenough, Tom Gross, Garth Heron, Malcolm Hill, Vince Hoban, Alan Hughes, Peter Johnston, Nora Kellock, John Lynch, Steve McGoldrick, Adam McLachlan, Vance McQueen, Andy Methven, Ian Millar,  Brian Murray, Hugh Newman, Paul Quay, Dennis Reay, Neil Roden, Colin Rutherford, John Ryan, Nick Schofield, Jim Schroedinger, David Shepherd, Alan Sinclair, Ian Smith, Stuart Smith, Jan Soderholm, Peter Taylor, Robbie Taylor, Richard Tinkler, George Turner and Pierre van Esch.

# Introduction

All we can be certain of is the requirement to change and implement best practice faster than our competitors. This means understanding and driving the dynamics of a business culture and tapping the ingenuity and creativity of our people. This requires men and women of strong vision and conviction who are prepared to tackle cultural issues from a behavioural perspective. This means you will be reading about, practising and applying techniques which many organisations are currently incapable of using effectively – because they do not have the quality of change leaders to successfully undertake them.

If you have read this far and the challenge of applying these techniques excites you to read more, you are one of the new genre of leaders determined to take responsibility for changing the future of their business. As you read, you will be able to apply the strategies and approaches within the book to our own unique business.I trust you will benefit personally from applying the approach.

The book gets its title because organisational culture is much misunderstood. The iceberg analogy is applied because corporate culture is perceived as being difficult to define, explain, assess and change. The mass of the iceberg is 'unseen' but powerful in directing its movements. Similarly, corporate culture is a powerful force which, when harnessed ,can be used to create incredible results for the people, for the business and for its customers. This book is about harnessing the power of the culture by providing strategies for radical improvement. At the heart of each chapter is the belief that change will come about only through mastering the potential of the organisation's most precious resource – its people.

The themes within the book are strongly behavioural in nature and are founded upon the belief that without leadership there is no change. Much of this book has come about from practical and effective consultancy interventions in many businesses since the publication of my book *Creating Culture Change* in 1990 and its revised and updated version in 1997. This book builds upon taking culture change to the next stage of thinking on implementation, addressing such core issues as Vision, Values, Mission, Leadership and Change itself. Therefore, a major theme is speed of implementation.

The book is directed towards dealing with the key issues that leaders in industry and commerce will have to confront in order to stay ahead of their competitors in the next ten years. Much of what is written is challenging by its very nature and will require managers to reappraise their contribution and commitment to driving change – for often, change starts with self. What follows in the chapters ahead will provide a comprehensive guide and checklist for the manager of change who is keen on championing change.

## The target audience for this book

Increasingly, managers are required to move beyond their individual technical specialism and become masters of change. The discussion of whether managers should be leaders is fast becoming exhausted. Many corporations are starting to understand that they need to move managers away from controlling resources to mastering transformations. This book is geared towards providing people at all levels with knowledge and motivation to use and implement the ideas within it. As a writing convenience in many instances I refer to people in the masculine form, but in all instances it applies to both sexes.

## Chapter outline

The chapters in this book outline in detail how cultures evolve and how they can be developed to become highly competitive businesses. Much of what is written is applicable to both public and private sectors.

Relevant research findings in corporate culture and 'best practice' from consultancy interventions is incorporated with key bullet points summarising the main issues at the end of each chapter.

Case studies in anecdotal form are enclosed to outline key practices.

**Chapter 1: Mastering Corporate Potential** squarely outlines the benefits, strategies and key issues which need to be addressed to start changing the culture of any organisation.

**Chapter 2: New Perspectives on Change** starts with the 'end in mind' and discusses ways to diagnose and action a new culture through the 9 S's framework.

**Chapter 3: The Challenge of Change** discusses communicating the benefits, rather than the features, of change and how to avoid cynicism towards change from all levels in the organisation.

**Chapter 4: Why 90% of Cultural Interventions fail** explores the effectiveness of cultural change programmes and look at ways to avoid pitfalls or disasters when instituting change.

**Chapter 5: Understanding Corporate Culture** explains the variety of cultures which exist within a company and the problems of failing to develop the most appropriate culture for the business.

**Chapter 6: The Cultural Iceberg** explains the dynamics of corporate culture and how to leverage change.

**Chapter 7: Vision, Mission, Values, Strategic Planning** outlines, clarifies and explains how these issues fit together, and how they have to be debated and shared with the top team and staff, in order to commit to action.

**Chapter 8 : Walking the talk – Leading Strategic Change** concentrates on key issues to develop Leaders from managers, focusing upon the transformational rather than the transactional nature of the role.

**Chapter 9 : Shaping the Strategic Leader** deals in some detail with the way personal values which shape behaviours are explained as well as outlining key skills and abilities required for the leader role.

**Chapter 10: The motivational calculus** explores the issue of applying motivational theory in a practical manner to win the support of all staff. It also highlights the action needed, and the preconditions necessary, to create an empowered culture.

**Chapter 11: Empowerment – in pursuit of the Holy Grail** provides the change maker with the conditions under which empowerment can flourish – strongly stating that empowerment is a condition which has to be grown rather than given.

**Chapter 12: Managing performance** focuses upon creating the right environment of trust in order to develop people effectively. The issues of managing poor performance and problem staff is an issue which managers should deal with, and occupies a significant element of the chapter.

**Chapter 13: Re-engineering a strong customer focus** firmly grasps the core issues which relate to reviewing and re-engineering the business to appeal to seamless customer service. The requirement for a strong culture to support the new structure and processes is outlined so, too, are talking through the customer service issues faced by many organisations.

**Chapter 14: Speed of Change – you're fast or you're dead** highlights the view that speed and responsiveness are essential elements of any successful business culture and outlines ten issues which need to be considered by organisations in the next ten years.

The book has been written to flow as a sequence but it is equally flexible to accommodate the examination of core issues. I hope you will use the book to support your thoughts on change. I would be delighted to hear how you progress.

Philip Atkinson © 1997
Transformations UK Ltd.
11 Alva St., Edinburgh
EH 2 4PH
Tel 0131-346-1276 /226-4519 fax 0131-346-1618
Email phil@transform.win-uk.net
Website www.lookhere.co.uk/transform/

*Chapter 1*

# Mastering Corporate Potential

*Many organisations fail to create a high performance team driven culture, which fulfils the potential of their people. This huge waste in terms of energy, enthusiasm, commitment and drive can be radically reduced by focusing on inspiring staff to move beyond their zone of comfort and commit to optimal performance. This book is about developing strategies to achieve this goal.*

## Strategies for maximising human potential

When you start to calculate how much is lost to any business through the application of archaic management principles, it is no surprise that many staff see their role as no more than a mundane 9-5 job which meets only their basic needs. So it's hardly surprising that the contribution and creativity displayed at work is not always of the highest level.

Few organisations understand the true financial cost to their business of failing to master the full potential of their people. It runs to billions of pounds and dollars each year in wasted energy, enthusiasm displayed but never tapped and lost opportunities for improvement. Even fewer organisations have come to terms with measuring the human cost and taking action. This text provides a structure to which you can adhere, one which will provide you with clear strategies to maximise the potential of your most important asset or resource – your people.

# Just imagine the business in which you work belongs to you

The quality of the service you provide in business is determined by the quality of your people. This, in turn, is determined by how they are managed. So just imagine the business in which you work belongs to you — the salaries and wages paid to staff come from your own pocket. Let's assume that as business expands and customer loyalty improves, your service is perceived as high 'value added', resulting in increased profits, personal gain and satisfaction. Now consider that if the service you offer is less than attractive, resulting in poor customer retention, there would be contraction, significant personal loss and, perhaps, business failure and bankruptcy. Bearing these scenarios in mind, ask yourself these questions:

**Would you manage people differently if your personal circumstances were impacted upon by their performance?**

**Why would you manage differently?**

**What current organisational and managerial issues, if resolved, could result in substantial business improvement?**

Often, I will start a training workshop by asking these three simple questions, which can promote a great deal of discussion. In the debate, blame is often shifted to others. For instance, people highlight "If it wasn't for my boss, I'd be able to do X". They do not see themselves as having the responsibility to affect and change the environment in which they work; this is all too common in organisations in which managers will not take on the responsibility to drive change.

To truly reap the benefits of getting the most from our people, the task is to get them to agree that they have some degree of responsibility for influencing the way in which they work. Once we agree that people should help others, either in a managerial or coaching context, we can start selling the idea that managing and leading people is a deliberate process — which can be learned and improved over time. And more importantly, it is the responsibility of every manager to help his or her team to excel and achieve their best.

*The feudal manager*

*The manager of a branch office in the automotive finance industry insisted that staff should refer to him and his two deputy managers as 'Mr'. On festive occasions, first names would be allowed. This created an interesting working climate. Car parking spaces were allocated only to the three senior managers. However, if a manager was away on business, a member of staff was allowed to use his space. But on several occasions staff were told to move their car because a manager's wife would be shopping in town and needed somewhere to park her car.*

*Questions for analysis*

*How willing do you think staff would be to share with the manager ideas for improving business performance?*

*How successful do you think empowerment would be in this business?*

*The team player*

*Another branch in the same business, employing about 30 people, is run by a young manager who insists on first name terms. He is approached by staff who have noticed that, at certain times of the week and in the summer months, there is a bottleneck and excessive 'queuing' on telephones in some administrative areas. He asks for their solution, which is cross-training of staff. The administrators, who process the work of the account managers, develop a manual and conduct one-on-one training with account managers. The account managers in turn, ensure that, to understand the importance of face-to-face customer care, administrators are introduced to all the car dealers in the area.*

> *Questions for analysis*
>
> *Ask yourself the same questions.*
>
> *How willing would staff be to share with their manager ideas for improving business performance?*
>
> *How successful do you think empowerment would be in this business?*
>
> *Answers to the two cases are radically different because the manager's style impacts positively or negatively on his people and the contribution they make.*

## Achieving results through others

People are the most important resource a company has to meets its objectives. How people are managed or led is critical in generating value added to any business. I would like to think the key role of any manager is to achieve results through the capabilities and skills of his or her people. I wonder how frequently managers, or members of an organisation's top team, see themselves investing in the future of their business by developing staff.

Providing education and improving the requisite skills, knowledge and attitudes of staff is critical for any business. But how often are people equipped just with the knowledge to perform technical or administrative aspects of their work, to the detriment of delivering beyond the extra mile? Investing in people is sometimes taken for granted and not viewed as a capital investment in business results and customer service.

Education does not refer solely to training. And although training can be a useful and powerful method of change, it is not always the most appropriate. Coaching, mentoring, one on one interventions, guided study, open learning and action learning and experiental learning are extremely powerful approaches to developing the individual. To really get to grips with the potential issues, ask yourself the following three questions:

# What do your staff do when they are not working for you?

Understanding the motivational drive of all staff who work with you, and seeing the individual as a person, is extremely important. Apart from making major contributions, individuals can stimulate innovative solutions to improve the performance of the business – as long as the culture enables them to do so.

I know a receptionist who is a part-time dance teacher. When teaching, she employs a great deal of motivation at a personal level, but has little opportunity to express these skills at work. So where is her creative energy directed? That's right: at the dance studio. This is an appalling waste of energy of which the receptionist's manager isn't even aware.

Managers should be encouraged to identify the talents that people bring to work. More importantly, they should think of innovative ways to apply the repertoire of abilities and competencies of employees at all levels of the business. Managers should deliberately focus attention on what drives each of their people to express innovative ideas and practices.

My experience is that people develop certain skills in context and apply their skills solely or often in 'context specific' situations. For instance, the member of the debating society will seek to improve his methods of communication and influence by attending weekly debating society sessions – continually applying and improving techniques. But, back in the organisation, in normal working hours, these skills are not applied or practised; they remain untapped. On initial examination, the job responsibilities may indicate there is little opportunity to use this skill in a specific role. But the question should be asked: how can we as an organisation make best use of this person's talents? What concerns me most is that when running cultural change workshops and selling the message of maximising potential, many managers are unaware of the abilities and experience of their staff – which may indicate they have little interest in the people working for them.

## How do staff demonstrate their resourcefulness when involved in in other activities not associated with work?

In whatever capacity staff are employed, they possess many capabilities outside their defined work role. This may be linked to their career or to the job they did before joining your organisation. Based on their experience, what contribution could they make to improve the performance of your business?

Often, members of staff have little opportunity to expand their horizon of activities. Yet they may have a great need to take charge and influence events. When we find out what occupies people's time outside work, we often see people volunteering to organise events and take on formidable responsibilities. I talked with a shop worker who was part-time director of a voluntary organisation committed to community welfare issues. The talents she displayed were organising voluntary and unpaid staff, managing a tight budget, winning support from the local community and negotiating for funds with local and central government agencies. These were probably never applied, tested or thought relevant for her paid employment. What a waste of talent and experience.

**Have we ever developed a full audit to assess staff experience outside the organisation?**

What experience and knowledge acquired by people working in other environments will help shape our business? Working with a large insurance sales organisation, I asked how often the company benchmarked practices of key competitors. A fairly non-committal response indicated they did not. We immediately set up a team of sales staff to examine the following:

- What training was given to staff on joining the business?

- Who provided the training and what were the key issues, products and markets to which attention was focused?

- What models were used to conceptualise the 'how to' sales process?

- What closing techniques were used?

- To which sales guru did they attribute their sales model? And what techniques were most powerful?

- How were sales organised in other companies? Was it by region, type of customer, product?

• How were people managed and what was the span of control?

• Which emerging issues will competitors' Sales staff address in the next six months?

By working through this process, the sales team did very little work outside their immediate circle of colleagues simply because so many members of the larger team had worked for competitors. They knew the systems, processes and techniques used on a day to day basis. Many sales staff even had copies of competitors' training manuals highlighting development activities. All this free information was helpful to the business. It just had to be unlocked.

Much information was available but hidden from view because no one had asked the right questions. The power of questions will generate untold returns. In this example, staff were constrained by their proximity to their most recent experience or job. They did not understand that much of what competitors were doing may work for the organisation as well as for them.

Just answering these three basic questions helps our understanding that we do not really capture the potentiality of our staff and their experience. We should start looking at what staff could achieve if encouraged to move beyond the limits of their present capabilities.

## Innovative thinking to stimulate the contribution of others

This requires a philosophy alien to many management teams who see development and training activities as an expense rather than an investment. The analogy with the emerging Third World nation which requires an injection into its educational infrastructure holds true for most organisations. Research into economic development of emerging countries suggests that the most important investment is in the educational infrastructure of that country. Doing so will move the present level of education from a very low to a moderate standard quite quickly. Significant further investment will provide that country with a comparative country advantage. One has only to make reference to the Pacific Rim and surrounding countries in Asia. Significant investment and a high intensity of focus, initially from Japan, now has become the norm for Korea, Indonesia and Malaysia and becoming a feature in

Vietnam, Thailand, China and the remaining Tiger economies. Educational standards far exceed many western economies including those of the UK and the US.

Looking at illiteracy rates in the UK and US I realise just how much we have fallen behind in the international commitment to education. If, nationally, education is not valued on a national 'must have' basis, what commitment is there to training and development in industry and commerce? Depending upon the industry and sector, there can be varying commitment to continuing development but there are still not enough signs that employers are taking the development issue seriously.

Apart from Third World countries with poor educational systems, there are Third World companies and organisations in which the role of education and development of people is a low priority. By investing and creating a strong infrastructure in an organisation, the contribution of people increases markedly. I have worked with businesses who failed dismally to induct their staff, even at the basic level, into what is required of them. I have also worked with companies who have failed to give sales staff the product knowledge and sell a wide range of products. Consequences of adopting a *laissez-faire* attitude to training and development can be dire. How can people contribute and add value when basic training in organisations' purpose, products and service is so poor? The training we envisage in this text exceeds the basics outlined. This training is essential to take organisations into the high performing category.

## Issues on development

### • Exposure to knowledge is not enough

Simple exposure to ideas and knowledge is not enough. For development to work, it is critical that staff see benefits or establish a need for acquiring and applying knowledge or skill in their day to day work. Telling people to attend a series of unrelated training modules may improve their short term recall of information but will do nothing for radical improvement in corporate performance.

### • Development activity bears no relation to actual work performed

Development activity is frequently not related to performance standards and day-to-day work. If the skill is not to be practised in the work environment and not integrated almost immediately after being introduced then it is highly unlikely to become part of that person's abilities and competencies.

## Human Potential Inventory

Very few organisations actually undertake what I would call a Human Potential Inventory. Many undertake a 'competencies' review for assessing salary and wage structures or job evaluation exercises to design a remuneration strategy. But very few move beyond the numbers game of manpower planning. Neither do they really value, map and document current experience and potential of their people or plan enhancement through a structured approach.

The average top teams would be shocked to find what organisations could achieve if employees were managed effectively and their people's potential fully realised. The results of such a survey or inventory are usually staggering because they highlight the positive role that the organisation must take to harness the energy inherent within its people. This is becoming a crisis area for organisations who have difficulty retaining staff with special knowledge or skills. Many companies, failing to see the oncoming crisis, continue to man their business from a skills market which is in short supply.

## Demographic downwave

This crisis is connected to 'baby boomers' coming of age and shifting social values associated with choice at a time of improved birth control and in which relationships other than marriage are becoming more acceptable. The result: a severe decline in the birth rate since 1973 .

This has impacted seriously on industry and commerce 20 years or so later, when fewer young people are looking for work. Coupled with this trend, and a decline in educational standards in real terms, commercial organisations want people who are specifically, rather than generally, educated.

Employers are increasingly more selective, so much so that a leading UK retailer announced they only employed 75% of required graduates for management positions because the quality on offer was below their standard. They would rather operate with fewer good quality people than with a full complement of people of varying quality. This trend may be industry specific but generally speaking human resources professionals are talking increasingly about the dearth of good quality candidates for a variety of positions at different levels.

Recently, I was involved with the recruitment and selection of an operations director for a major business There were more than 200 replies to an advert in *The Times* — but too few of those applying had the qualifications, experience and drive to benefit the business. Of six candidates suitable for interview, only three showed up. The others had been offered positions in other companies.

This is a common occurrence. There is a sharp deficit between demand and supply for good quality staff. Organisations need to develop innovative strategies to attract excellent candidates and develop staff.

## Demography impacting upon corporate performance

With fewer people available, organisations are competing head on for quality candidates. So there is a crisis in many industries and many business sectors. The quality of staff in critical positions in these businesses will determine the results they achieve. Organisations are competing in their own industry, and with other industries for the same people.

With good quality, high calibre candidates in short supply, they have the pick of 'quality' employers. Increasingly, we are finding that candidates for key positions and will only commit to a business in which they believe they can enhance their experience, display their creativity and be given an opportunity to grow.

In recent months I have been asked by several companies for:

• Candidates to fulfil the role of Total Quality director.

• Sales staff who can interact, influence and sell insurance services — for which there is a huge demand throughout the industry.

• Managers to lead cross-functional teams in financial service sales, customer-focused teams in banks, managers to lead technical services and IT managers focused upon implementation.

Recruiting companies have experienced major problems in recruiting staff. These problems are further exacerbated as a result of regional or commercial demand in one or several areas. This is a big issue which many organisations have not confronted.

I see this becoming a major problem and a critical issue – an emerging trend throughout the UK, Europe and North America. Among the issues which top teams need to address:

- Some organisations are still not aware of the decline in supply of good quality candidates.

- Some organisations do not know how to attract people of the right calibre.

- Many organisations have not grasped the opportunities, nor developed conditions which would attract candidates to the business.

- Retention through meaningful career development is critical. If opportunities are not created for advancement and experience building, candidates will find other employers willing to offer such opportunities.

For instance, in recent years the following practices have become clear in forming employment relationships.

- In the oil industry, some employers are offering employment terms to successful candidates of at least two foreign placements. In this way newly-appointed graduate trainees gain overseas experience in their first 18 months of employment.

- Financial services firms are offering sponsored opportunities to learn languages and undertake MBAs.

- Home working, with the provision of personal computers, telecommunications and all required technology to part-time staff in a variety of businesses.

Organisations which value the contribution of core staff have had to develop innovative policies to generate sufficient interest in their companies. These policies are designed to attract, and retain, candidates.

## Where does our organisation stand in mastering the potential stakes?

Key issues need to be resolved in order to master the potential of staff. The exercise which follows is critical for any top team. To generate powerful results, I use a variant of this exercise, together with other tools and techniques.

There follows an analysis that can be conducted at an organisational, functional, departmental or team level. I have even used it when I appraised competencies displayed in a re-engineered customer focus process. This helped identify how to bridge the gap between 'now' competencies and future requirements.

List the people you are going to assess and agree on the core competencies in a general sense. This may include their current knowledge, their ability to develop the required experience, their current motivation and other circumstances. Now appraise them on current performance illustrated on the horizontal scale in the diagram. You may want to rely on your judgement and use a one to ten scale with ten as 'high degree of competence'.

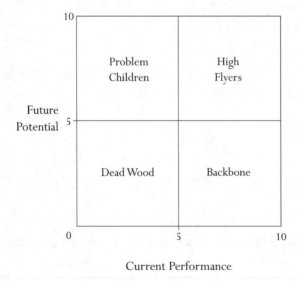

*Diagram 1. The four quadrant model*

Now comes the interesting part. You will have to make subjective assessments and use your experience and judgement.

Decide where you would place these same people in terms of their potential contribution to the business (vertical scale). Now you have two co-ordinates and can plot each individual on the grid. This is a very simple and subjective assessment in which – importantly – managers express their real views on staff. It's better to discuss subjective perceptions and then agree objective criteria for further debate. We have now arrived at a method of assessing how people fit into the four quadrant model. Applied at various levels, this promotes interesting questions about the action needed to proceed.

## Dead wood

An unfortunate term which implies a person is performing below requirements and does not appear to have potential. Some issues are obvious – why are they defined as dead wood and deemed to be of little value to the organisation? I firmly believe you get the staff you deserve. So if you have identified a sizeable number of poor performers, why are they there and why has action not been taken? What steps need to be taken to ensure the person satisfies at least the basic criteria of the job? A variety of issues must be debated. Does the person have the requisite administrative or technical knowledge but is lacking in other skill areas? What specifically lets them down and what can you do to help them meet the criteria of acceptable performance?

There is a further need to explore the perceptions shared by others and to agree objective criteria which would indicate why an individual fits in the lower left hand quadrant. (Please note that this is important for all four positions of the grid.)

## 'Problem children'

'Problem children' are usually people who have moved to new positions or whose roles may have changed. They may or may not realise they can no longer depend solely upon technical specialism or administrative capabilities – they may be lost in their role. Re-equipping staff with capabilities to stretch beyond the 'technical' is the issue. So focus on staff who have not made the transition. This could include staff who have just been promoted or who have changed their job and are ill-prepared to deal with their new role.

˜ In the 70s many staff who were the 'backbone' of the business suddenly became 'problem children' because new technology had been introduced. Their role had changed and minimal support was given to help drive them up the learning curve.

People with a highly technical background sometimes fit within this quadrant, especially when they are given their first new managerial position. They may realise they need to develop new skills and abilities but there may be a 'disconnect' between the time needed to learn new skills and actually doing the job. The result is they have to learn 'on the job' which can be extremely frustrating. Ill prepared people can find a change in their role distressful. Abilities to do a new job or fulfil a new role well do not materialise by magic.

If time is invested in 'problem children' they can flourish. If it is not, they may revert to the limits of their technical or operational background. If totally neglected, they will fall into the 'dead wood' area and probably display little interest in their job. They will either stay in their job because they cannot find anything else, or perform to a minimum standard.

## 98% of people come to work to do a good job

People who manage others must realise that skills and motivations displayed by their team are a reflection of the management style of their boss. No-one wants to be seen as 'dead wood' or a 'problem child' – we need a positive image of ourselves. This happens to people because others fail to clarify expectations and then resource the required development. I believe the vast majority of people come to work to do a good job. No-one wants to be branded below standard but if managers took their people development role seriously, under-performing staff would be fully aware. I have no doubt that when most people are told they are not performing the vast majority take decisive action to improve.

Performance issues should be addressed by communication, coaching and honest feedback of bad news. Once people are aware of what is required, most will commit to improve.

## The backbone

These people have extensive experience which takes them outside their technical comfort zone. They have stretched and work across boundaries. They have learnt to do things in different ways and probably work with others from different areas. They may never be high performers but they are dependable, trustworthy and an asset to the business and their colleagues. How they have developed is of high value and if developed further they could move up to the 'high flyer' quadrant. If, of course, there are too many staff in this category, the organisation may stagnate.

In too many organisations there is a plethora of such people in this quadrant. It indicates that the organisation is not really moving forward, just doing the 'same old stuff'. To move and compete requires new beliefs, a new way of thinking that people can learn more, that they can be developed, that there is a host of experience which could be used more effectively. Learning does not stop when a person has been in the same position for some years or has more grey hair and years of service than his or her colleagues. Learning to use established skills and additionally develop new skills can move everyone into the top right hand quadrant.

# High performers

These people are excellent at what they do. Being a high performer can relate to any position or function, whether clerical or middle management. High performers have perfected their ability to work with others and constantly look for challenges. All staff have the potential to become high performers.

The term 'high performers' does not suggest an elite group it refers to 'being all you can be'. The diagram of four quadrants on page 28 are specific to a job or role and it is the role of managers to resource and support the organisation with the ability to get all their staff into this quadrant.

The determining factor is how well an organisation values its people and the direct action of managers to create an excellent organisation.

# Cause and effect – the real problem

Where is the real barrier to creating excellence? It resides in the actions (or rather inactions) of executive managers. The cause may be found in circumstances in which they are afraid to take the first step – consider changing the way they do things.

# The cause effect equation CAUSE = EFFECT

Where are your staff in the cause – effect equation? There are those who believe they are in the right hand side of the equation. They are at 'effect'. They believe that what they are is caused by others outside their control and they are the result. They do not take responsibility for the process of improvement. When people are at 'effect', they believe they are at the result of someone else's actions. When they are at 'cause', they recognise that they have the responsibility to grow and develop. Until we can win the support of our top teams to lead and encourage others to take responsibility and be at 'cause', we will only be tinkering with sub-system change.

## Summary and bullet points

It is critical that organisations in the public and private sector take note of these issues. Mastering the potential of their people = mastering the potential of their business.

People bring talents, experiences, aptitudes, competencies and attitudes to their business. We probably only tap 50% of their potential. The other 50% is wasted or untapped – but expressed elsewhere, probably when pursuing activities outside their full time (or even part-time) employment.

It is the responsibility of the person who manages people to get the most from them, but this can only be done with top team commitment. This says much about creating a dominant, positive and deliberate management style. Further chapters will highlight the strategies which can be taken to master the potential of the most valuable resource of your business – your people.

- Assume the role of business owner. What would you do to master the potential of your people?

- What organisational issues are stopping your organisation getting the most from its people?

- The quality of the manager, and his or her values, determines the climate for learning and stretching.

- Managers are usually paid not because they are invaluable geniuses but because they are focused on getting results through others.

- What do your staff do when they are not working for you?

- Ensure you commit to providing a culture in which staff can display their creativity in business hours.

- Tap in to how staff can use their resourcefulness to further boost your business.

- Develop a human potential inventory of staff experiences, interests, competencies and aspirations.

- Commit to a rounded and rigorous development process.

- If you are at the consequence of the demographic downwave, or about to be affected by short supply of talented people, create effective staff selection and retention policies throughout the business.

- Most employees choose their employer — not the other way around.

- Assess where your staff reside on the potential -performance grid. Then assess where others would plot your own performance.

- Ensure your strategies are promoting a balance of organisational and self responsibility to be at the 'cause' side of the cause = effect equation.

# *Chapter 2:*

# New Perspectives on Change

Having the capacity to change, and do so speedily and seamlessy, is the most dominant factor in separating the high performing business from poorer competitors. Knowing how to develop this 'culture', or way of working, is central to any business. The top team which commits to an initiative with this as its ultimate goal will reap rewards from the marketplace. Understanding that change in the market, in customer demands and new technology will increase in intensity and complexity, demands that organisations develop the internal capacity to anticipate and master the process of change. Transforming the business will come about through design, rather than by default or accident. Understanding that processes can be harnessed to make 'change' a friend rather than foe is central to the purpose of this book, which is to ease transitions through understanding and shaping your organisational culture to meet and master the demands of the new century.

## Vision : Start with the end in mind

It is critical to shape a vision of what you want your culture to be. So now we will start the process of mastering steps to corporate excellence. This means viewing change from several perspectives.

*Imagine that change in your organisation is a natural, evolving process which is actively welcomed by all. To what changes would you commit, knowing you could not fail?*

I want to ensure you use this text as a tool and methodology to achieve the core steps to successful change. To achieve this goal let's start with the end in mind and imagine a strong corporate culture where change is the norm. To enter the spirit of this exercise, I want to establish the degree of commitment and action necessary to move from where you are to where you want to be. I want to manage the gap in the culture and, in order to do so, need you to commit to writing down the top five changes you would like to see.

It may help to write down the changes you would desire right now and consider the impact these changes would have on the performance of your business. Writing down how you want things to be is an extremely valuable exercise because, too often, ideas for improvement remain in the heads of managers, never to be committed to paper. Once in some tangible form, they can be shaped and acted upon. So please commit those thoughts now by copying and using the chart below.

| | Changes | Consequences for the Business |
|---|---|---|
| 1. | | |
| 2. | | |
| 3. | | |
| 4. | | |
| 5. | | |

Table 1. Changes you want to see

You might want to focus on the core benefits attributed to the business, rather than the features of implementation. That can come later. What is really important is that you and your colleagues share a vision for the future. Achieving that vision will be the strategy for implementation which will evolve from your thinking. And thinking is a creative process in which there are no constraints, no self-limiting beliefs to cloud your judgement about what your organisation will achieve.

## All you are, have and become started with a vision

The benefits of thinking differently about shaping your culture are really appreciated when you test for understanding with your colleagues and peers. Sharing visions and dreams is probably understated in managerial competencies of top players because they are so adept and well practised at questioning and evaluating everything. To prove this, look at a personal example. Think through and examine how you have shaped your personal circumstances, the relationships and family of which you are part. Think of your material possessions, the house in which you live and all those activities in which you engage. Think of your partner, your children, your car, your holidays and remember they all started out as a dream or personal vision. Just as you can shape your personal visions into reality, you can shape the corporate culture by starting with a vision. Removing the self-imposed barriers by asking the question 'if you knew you could not fail' gives meaning to building a strong culture.

This is great as a starter activity and you may want to give a great deal more thought to the process To do this requires an analysis of your culture. Understanding the dynamics of culture is dealt with in Step 2, but for now it is important to look at a neat classification system which will help you think through the core cultural issues.

## The 9 S's Framework*

This framework will aid and clarify the future vision for the business. It is based upon the premise that the culture of the business can be analysed in terms of hard tangible factors and softer elements which are just as enduring but more difficult to define. Based upon the model, the 9 S's are neatly defined into Hard and Soft S's.

* See *Creating Culture Change* for a more detailed analysis.

*Strategy: knowing and communicating*

*Having developed a great strategy for the business, it is unhelpful to keep it locked in a black box. Of equal importance is communication of the strategy to all employees.*

*There is a test I apply to a company when I first meet staff. I ask many open-ended questions to find out where the company is going and what plans it has for the future. My interest is purely how well the top team has communicated the vision for the business into tangible actions of staff at all levels. In companies where the vision is shared, at even a basic level, it is usually a strong indicator that staff are valued. They are valued because they have become part of the process. I know of no other way of aligning people who work with me than sharing my visions of where the business is going, so that I can align their interests, motivations and talents on that same mission.*

The Hard S's are sometimes described as concrete elements of the business which are easily understood. For instance, the strategy, goals, directions, stated objectives, structure, method of allocating key roles and responsibilities to those who drive the business, and systems, procedures, protocols and processes which determine how roles and responsibilities are undertaken. The level of analysis that follows can relate to how well these three Hard S's are achieved. This can easily be assessed. But the real thrust comes when we examine the degree to which each of these factors needs to change to what is 'desired.' Many managers, directors and top team players have never really thought through this level of analysis in terms of understanding their business culture. When they use this tool, they are able to isolate those factors which need to be radically improved. This methodology is particularly powerful because it enables top team members to share perceptions with those in the business who operate from a different perspective. It also is considered powerful because it enables managers to state their perceptions when defining the vision in tangible terms. Making the vision more tangible and specific focuses the 'behaviours' which need to be practised consistently by managers to achieve the end goal. (A detailed questionnaire analysis which enables a Cultural Survey to be completed.)

## The Soft S's

The Soft S's relate to aspects of the business which are more difficult to define. Interestingly, though, they may have a much more powerful impact upon business performance than any of the Hard S's. For instance, the style of management portrayed may exist by default or accident but can be extremely effective in winning the hearts and minds of staff to perform beyond the call of duty. A really enthusiastic manager who truly believes in empowering staff to take responsibility for implementing solutions can have a more direct impact on creating positive morale than any system or protocol. And often the lack of strategic direction can be compensated for in some instances by the shared value of cross-functional working. The four core Soft S's include style of management, which should not be left to chance. It's important that we agree how to manage people and resources. All that style does is help us to apply the most appropriate and powerful approach when working with people.

---

*Symbols: control through space*

*In many organisations, the size of the executive's mahogany desk and the size of his or her office tells us what is important and what is not. In one financial services company the prestige a manager enjoyed was determined by desk size and office decor. Maintenance of these old-fashioned status symbols made it almost impossible to convince employees that 'empowerment' was to become a dominant value of the business. The basic conflict was represented by status differences in how managers were physically accommodated compared with the weak message communicated to staff lacking credibility.*

*Conversely, the managing director of another financial services company regularly lunched with staff in the company canteen and insisted on first name terms at all times.*

---

The degree of motivation and commitment displayed by staff is a direct result of how people are managed. Competencies brought together by staff are reflected in their acquisition and application of skills. People in the enterprise are bound by the values of the business – those things which are accepted as the fabric which holds people together in a common mission.

Symbols are representations of dominant aspects of the culture and can range from the public profile of the business to allocation rewards based upon seniority and/or contribution.

An additional S factor which operates between the Hard and Soft S's is best described as a flux or glue which holds everything together. Synergy, the teamwork that unites diverse groups and brings commitment to a goal, is best reflected in problem-solving and corrective action. Often displayed during a crisis, it says more about how the business is run than any other factor.

For instance, it is strongly encouraged that a number of levels of analysis are conducted when using the 9 S framework. Frequently, top team members test their own perception of where they currently stand in the 9 S stakes. The true image emerges when this perception is tested with that of other key constituents of the processes – staff at other levels and locations and customers, who buy the company products. Undertaking this level of analysis, critical in shaping the desired vision, improves the understanding of the perceptions of others with a stake in the business.

Even more important is ensuring that debate focuses clearly on firstly agreeing the accuracy of 'what is.' Until this is agreed, continuation of the exercise is pointless. However, some analysts would suggest the vast majority of businesses fail to measure and define the 'what is' state of their business culture. By undertaking the exercise, the result is a complete learning experience. Failing to agree on the current state of culture confuses direction for improvement, frustrates managers at lower levels and highlights that there is little agreement on a 'shared vision' of action needed to achieve a highly refined 'desired' culture.

Looking through Table 2, it is possible to test for understanding on a number of levels. Companies we have worked with found that this rudimentary exercise yielded positive results – the foundation for significant improvement. Different levels of management can be carefully forged together to align their interests and direct their energies towards achieving standards far above their expectations.

The exercise is as follows:

# Cultural Assessment

Please give thought to the culture of the business. Culture generally depicts the 'way things are done around here'. It is important that your perception is accurate so please be honest in your response. Complete the grid below, identifying words or phrases which best illustrate each characteristic of the culture. Please complete the 'desired' component, focusing on what could be.

| Characteristic | Currently 'as is' | 'Desired' culture |
|---|---|---|
| **Strategy:** direction, goals, stated objectives | | |
| **Structures:** levels, management, core roles and responsibilities | | |
| **Systems:** rules, formalised agreements, systems, processes which determine 'how' work is completed. | | |
| **Symbols:** artefacts which signal what is important from that which is not | | |
| **Style:** How people are managed and led | | |
| **Staff:** the worth and value of people, communication | | |
| **Skills:** requisite attitudes, skills and knowledge, mix and competencies | | |
| **Shared Values:** those things which bind people together, a shared philosophy | | |
| **Synergy:** deliberate attempts to align constituents with processes. | | |

*Table 2. Cultural assessment*

Needless to say, this exercise is valuable in identifying key issues which need to be debated. The following format should be considered:

- Assess the culture 'as is' and share perceptions with key constituents.

- Understand what causes the culture to be 'as is'. This requires understanding the dynamics of causal relationships.

- Identify the vision or 'desired' culture and debate differences of perceptions. This requires discussing assumptions behind perceptions.

- Agree action to be taken to move from 'as is' to 'desired'

The final step is the most difficult of the process because it requires careful debate and a strong focus upon listening and testing for understanding amongst top team players.

## Preconditions for the cultural shift exercise

Before you commit to this exercise, it is important to work through what you really want to change and focus upon specifics. This is one of the areas in which companies make mistakes when engaging on a change initiative. Senior managers commit time and thought to the latest quick fix. They go through major features of the programme but fail to spend time defining specifically the end or 'desired' state for the company. One of the many reasons for this behaviour is a blind trust that changing the culture might sound and look right – the right thing to do without specific aims in mind. Managers may be unaware of causal relationships in the culture. Part of this analysis is discussed when we move to step two.

Conscious attention upon elements within the culture are musts for change. Without a compelling vision of a 'desired future state', it is unlikely that playing with the culture – almost by accident than design – will create the high performance business required to operate, dominate and compete. Any commitment to corporate performance which falls short of this ideal is of little value to customers, staff, those who drive the business and shareholders.

# Summary and bullet points

Step one of examining business culture is completed when there is full commitment to the need for change. This becomes evident when we understand what we are changing 'from' and to what we 'desire' to change.

Diagnosing the culture from one perspective is too limiting – you need to take perceptions of others into account. Failing to do so will generate a 'self-fulfilling prophecy' which is not based upon reality.

- Start with the end in mind. If you don't know where you are going, how does anybody else?

- Build a powerful vision. Ask for and listen to the vision of others at every level. Remember everyone has a valid view; creativity is not the sole preserve of top team members.

- Test for understanding.

- Dump all self-limiting beliefs which inhibit the excitement and possibility of the vision.

- Characterise culture through the 9 S's.

- Rigorously apply the 9 S model – you can generate far more detail and examine hindering factors when you devote time to planning for new possibilities.

- Develop the top team's abilities to break through any self-limiting beliefs about the business.

- Seriously commit to creative strategic thought and break through self-imposed barriers of rigid, logical thinking.

- Understand that business cultures can be created, designed and shaped.

- Understand that 98% of business cultures evolve by accident rather than design.

- Take charge to encourage others to share the vision for the culture

- Recognise that a strong competitive edge is achieved by developing the internal capability to master and implement change faster than your competitors.

# Chapter 3 :

# The Challenge of Change

This chapter focuses on major change management issues which impact upon most businesses. Challenging assertions in the next few pages may encourage you to think differently about how to go about changing your business.

When I work with companies on implementing change initiatives one of the first things I do is to work out who is 'for' the change and who is 'against' it. Culture change is a little bit like pregnancy. You can't be half pregnant. Either you are or you are not. It's the same with culture change. There's no sitting on the fence — either you are for it or against it.

Ostensibly there are two camps in the change process. The role of the change agent is to align interests and bring people together to commit to required changes. This means winning the support of those who think change is unnecessary. Part of this process is concerned with convincing others that benefits accrue from change. Often organisations engage themselves in change initiatives without telling staff why they are doing it. These companies have failed to reinforce with their most precious resource that there is a sound, sane and rational reason why the company or organisation is set out to improve performance. If most top team members stood back and explained to staff the benefits of the change process, they would probably discover that most people 'buy in' to the process.

## Features and benefits

In any selling or exercise where influence is required, it is far more productive to sell the benefits of change rather than the features. Yet many businesses fail to do this. If an organisation engages in an initiative in which substantial change is required, it is a wise investment to test the understanding of their people.

**45**

In a major international genetics business the chief executive and his principal officers agreed to run briefing sessions, explaining to staff why they had engaged on a cultural change programme. Even more importantly, when they conducted a cultural survey, they took time to share the results with staff. Taking things a stage further, they worked with staff to reappraise the core values which would drive the business well into the next century. These re-appraisals helped with the development of a role model of desired behaviours to be projected by core managers. Needless to say, commitment to the drive for change was strong and evident at all levels. Commitment was strong because the top team did not assume their people would work out the reasons for change themselves. They realised it was important to talk through and share reasons and to explain how the company was going to operate.

## Continued vigilance of the need to change

Amazingly, there can still be emphasis on selling a change programme rather than on the reasons why a company is pursuing change. Focusing on the customer as the driving force, or competitive forces, requiring radical improvement are issues reinforced by really successful companies. General Electric is one of the largest, most successful and profitable companies in the world – but does the chief executive sit back and bask in the glory? No. He and his team pursue the approach that if you are not getting better every day in every way, you are probably standing still. And if you are standing still, then in all probability your business is slipping backwards. There is a continual drive for being number one or two in every GE business. This continual drive, with customer service and quality at the forefront, will ensure the company maintains its dominant market position. How many other companies could learn from this model? You may wish to consider the dynamics of change in your own organisation by asking probing questions.

- **What weaknesses exist within your organisation?**

- **What competitor strategy could seriously disadvantage your business?**

- **What is the worst thing your core customers could do to your business?**

- **How well do your top team members understand and communicate the need for change?**

First, it is important to sell the message that change is important and natural. Second, the format to do so must focus on real reasons for change.

The diagram below should help to encourage the management group to work through threats to, and opportunities for the business. These can be perceived in the short and the long term. By devoting and investing time to this profile, it is possible to highlight reasons for required change and communicate those reasons to all staff.

|  | Threat | Opportunity |
|---|---|---|
| **Short term** | | |
| **Long term** | | |

Diagram 2. Threat and opportunity matrix

## Pessimistic behaviour

When communicating change, optimistic staff members will see the benefits of improving and moving from their comfort zone. The optimists see change as a positive challenge and a necessary aspect of improvement for the business and its people. Pessimists, on the other hand, fear the very nature of change itself. To pessimists, the word change seems to encourage a lack of control and breeds negative behaviours. Positive action is required to dismiss this viewpoint.

## Selling change

One of the most important jobs a chief executive and his or her top team have in the change process is reinforcement of the need to change, the need to grow. Investment in any activity to sell the 'desirability' of change will pay dividends. The role of the change agent or facilitator is to address change and influence others to look upon change as a natural process and an exciting challenge.

Those who are driving the process of change need to develop strategies which will lead to countering those who always seem to find ways to make good ideas fail. This is a reality of organisational life, the biggest challenge that many management teams will face. Before we go any further, we need to address this scepticism towards change, then take steps to destroy it. What conditions underpin the negative views held by some? Only after asking critical questions can we counter with new ways to sell the process of change.

For many organisations, this strategy is new . Gone is the day when change was introduced by decree, order and dictat. In order to win the support of people and utilise their potential, we have to adopt different values. We should start by focusing on changing through influence and persuasion. But let's understand why people are generally pessimistic in outlook and what conditions have created this negativity towards change.

## Self Assess your corporate programmes

Ask yourself about corporate programmes which come and go. What percentage really stood a chance of implementation? Apply the reality test. What really happened and why? As an experienced manager, you may well have seen many initiatives die. Such programmes, each with their own identity, range from customer care through to corporate excellence.

If you don't believe this, go to any manager's office and look at their bookshelves. Look at the corporate mementos proudly proclaiming initiative or attendance certificates. Take a random sample of your colleagues and ask them to list programmes that have been introduced. Once you have compiled the list, assess them on a ten point scale, with 1-2 as ineffective and 8-9-10 as effectively implemented. How many programmes flourished, changed working practices and promoted a strong customer service orientation? How many filtered through all levels of management and became business as usual? What percentage of programmes withered and died within a fairly short time, reinforcing the belief that the programme was a nine-day wonder, the latest quick fix?

## Great message, poorly sustained

To get a really good flavour of why scepticism can be rife, take a deeper look at the content of these programmes. One way to do this is by reading through training materials.

As you read, you will hit on gems that would make work more effective, provide added value, promote involvement and fun. You will undoubtedly uncover some really good ideas. You may come across tools and methodologies which remain in the confines of the book. You may want to consider why these approaches were never effectively implemented.

I recently undertook this exercise with senior staff in a major bank. I wanted to illustrate that the best intentions of some change initiatives are not always achieved. We went through folders relating to past change initiatives involving customer care, Quality Circles and Total Quality and came across the completion of action plans generated by a middle management group. It was suggested that 'mystery shopping' should be extended to all business customers, that sales executives should develop their own regional strategy and that briefing groups be implemented throughout the branch network. A few of these ideas had filtered through in some areas of the bank but were not evident in others

If these action plan notes had been implemented enthusiastically, they would have driven customer focus and contributed in the medium term to bottom line results. For some reason, the drive for change lost momentum or there was not enough time to implement the changes. Of greater concern, issues that had been identified as central in helping to improve business performance, were still unresolved.

## Time and energy wasted

It could be said there is never enough time to do what you really want. It's interesting to look not just at lost opportunities in terms of issues which should have been resolved, but at the energy expended by staff in thinking through and committing, at least initially, to the process of improvement. You may wonder how much time was wasted on these initiatives. Don't count the waste in pounds or dollars because there is a far greater cost — one which fuels the scepticism about change. Assess the time invested by people in training workshops and beyond, the time given freely to work on projects. Think through the enthusiasm portrayed by staff. Consider the optimism and the opportunity to really contribute and make a difference. Think of the promises made and not fulfilled. What effect did the launch of these projects have on the hearts and minds of those who make the organisation tick? How did it fashion their thinking about change? How does their view on change differ from those who are expert at implementing change?

## The really great companies

There are many large, good quality businesses which really drive the process of change. They learn from their mistakes and implement corrective and preventative action. General Electric, British Telecom, Marks & Spencer and many other excellent companies are thriving on change, sticking with change and becoming even better at implementing change.

In comparison, too many companies are stuck in their comfort zones; they change at a much slower rate, a rate which is not fast enough for survival. Let us concentrate upon this issue. How would you rate the top team's capability to manage change?

• **Do you have managers or senior officers who commit and take action? Or do they procrastinate and halt progress?**

• **Does your management team make the decision to change only when events leave them no alternative?**

• **Are your business leaders fast, flexible and driven by customer needs?**

• **Do they encourage flexibility, destroy bureaucratic practices and customer focus?**

- Do they encourage working across divisional boundaries and do they thrive on upward communication?

- Do your business leaders question everything in detail and fail to understand the bigger picture?

- Do they focus 95% of their available time upon studying, measuring and logging performance and spend only 5% implementing ideas?

- Do they question the need for change?

- Do they put things off? Do senior managers always find a reason not to do something?

Make no mistake, the capacity of the top team to lead and drive change is central to corporate survival. Answers to these questions illustrate how committed they are to the change process. Change is a serious business. A top team can either transform a business or can tinker at the edges.

## Corporate myth: people hate change

Change is a serious business, understood by too few people. Allow me to let you into a secret. People love change if they are involved in the process. If control resides with others, they will resist it. If we empower people to drive the change process, working with their views, their aspirations and needs clearly in mind, change would be viewed as a partnership.

## Thriving on change

When we see how people have been poorly managed it is hardly surprising that change is not always welcomed. This humorous example, which was provided by a client, refers to a group of managers within his own financial services business.

**A middle manager in corporate services obtained his degree 21 years ago. Since then, he has not opened a management journal. He thinks management development is the latest Charles Atlas course for managers;**

or catching the last five minutes of John Harvey Jones on a televised visit to a company in dire need of rejuvenation. Worse still, he left a time management workshop because something urgent came up.

More seriously, people like this work in your organisation. They are typical of middle management because top management have never taken seriously the need to change the organisation's style of management.

In our example the middle manager is happy to progress up the next level of management. He feels he can predict with certainty the scope of work he will perform and even influence the variety and intensity of his workload.

He may see himself seeking further security on a career path gently drifting onwards and upwards. He puts a great deal of faith in maintaining his technical specialism. The more mystery the better; the deeper and more technical the manager, the better the manager. This corporate belief in the sanctity of technical specialism to the detriment of change management has led to many business failures.

What makes the technical superiority theory lack credibility is that those organisations which foster this approach soon hamper the variety and ability to innovate and change. Our research shows that things are made worse by organisations which continually reinforce this behaviour through recognition and reward systems. Predictably, this type of manager is probably not going to take change seriously, especially when it impacts upon him and how he does his work. Those who have relied on technical expertise to create their position are hardly likely to encourage new ways of working, especially in areas in which they are comparatively ill-informed.

How does this person react when change is required to benefit the business? His commitment to change is, at best, half-hearted. He will examine and implement new ways of behaviour, because the content of his job has always been important.

This is reality in many organisations. Ask yourself:

- **How many colleagues at different levels of management display these characteristics?**

- **In how many ways do organisations encourage these practices?**

# A strategic view on the wisdom of change

Single-mindedness can be defined as when someone persistently displays the same behaviour and honestly expects to achieve a different result. Persistently applying the old approaches yields nothing but a tired, inappropriate result. The old ways of working no longer operate, but managers still do things the old way hoping new results will come about. When these efforts fail, many start putting more effort into the process and try even harder. Forcing a round peg into a square hole does not work. Employees need to learn and think in new ways. A new mindset is required. Using old ways to solve current problems is not sensible behaviour.

Sagacity is when we are sufficiently flexible to look at new ways to operate and improve. Single-mindedness creates a steady state of no improvement. Sagacity requires a self-critical attitude with feedback and adjustment to behaviour based upon interactions with others. You might want to ask about the the wise or the intransigent practices which managers display in their day-to-day work.

- **What does not work, but is still a major way of doing things in your organisation?**

- **What could work for the business but is counter to the mindset of the prevailing culture?**

- **What restrictive beliefs about how we manage hold us back from trying new ways?**

Answers to these questions support the need to start with top down interventions first. That will help us understand the scepticism and cynicism at lower levels.

# Destroy the cynicism at middle management level

When addressing large numbers of managers in workshops or projects, trainers find there are occasions on which people don't like their guiding values and beliefs about their management style to be challenged. However, it is only by challenging our way of working that performance is further improved. If sports coaches failed to challenge, the performance of players or athletes would be lacklustre and their careers short.

Apply the same doctrine to a group of managers and you could be in for a hard time. It is natural to defend one's viewpoint but when this becomes standard behaviour it is time to encourage managers to look in the mirror.

It is important that, when looking at new ways of working, prejudices must be challenged rather than reinforced. It is important to look at the dominant beliefs held by the manager and see how they gel with emerging and new core beliefs which will help the business to become more effective.

When outdated corporate and managerial beliefs are questioned, cynicism emerges. The first step is to destroy the cynicism at middle management levels and the only route is through the actions of those who drive the business – the top team. If we fail to achieve this, we will encounter the problems in the following paragraph.

The oft quoted remark, '90% of culture change or quality initiatives will fail' is attributed to lack of support and direction from those most senior in organisations. There are many reasons for failure. By understanding why failure occurs, positive action can be taken to ensure that '100% of initiatives will succeed'.

## Great theory – lousy implementation

One of the main reasons why variants of culture change fail is that insufficient effort goes into implementation. The concept of culture and change is explained and educational workshops arranged, often with a massive training input. But the effectiveness is in question. No real change takes place. Training by itself simply does not work – not without the support from those at the top. In too many instances, those attending programmes and courses learn how and why to do things but leave the session without commitment.

Any meaningful training event has to reflect what will happen in the future. If training fails to supply those attending with 'hands on' skills and abilities to do things differently, it has been merely academic. Further, if the behaviours identified as being important in the training event are not practised by senior management, why should anyone else take them seriously?

## Take decisive action

Change requires activity. Without action there is no improvement. Workshops have to be interactive events at which actions and responsibilities for change are agreed.

Meetings should not be talking shops debating theory, but structured so that change is introduced by the most senior people in the business. Action plans should be seen to be real and where those attending should be assured that progress will be monitored. If there is no clear plan for implementation, the sessions will have little impact or effect.

## System change does not equate to culture change

Before moving to specific elements of failure, it is useful to address the main stumbling blocks to implementation. Too many programmes for change rely almost entirely on changing strategy, structure and systems. This is a popular approach to introducing change. Many believe the cornerstone of quality is systems based. Far too many organisations have put their faith solely in achieving ISO 9000 or BS5750. This is the extent of their commitment to Quality. Achieving this standard, however important it is, will not go very far to creating a cultural change. It does not matter how much energy is put into systems and procedures – they do not create a strong value system devoted to customer service and empowerment.

A quality culture is one in which managers lead through teamwork, one in which a dominant culture of participation, continuous improvement and empowerment is the way things are achieved. To create this culture requires a major shift in behaviour, attitude, style and communication.

No standards, however positive, can promote changes in managerial behaviour. Culture, values and style can be fashioned only through the effort, commitment and action of those who run the company. Shaping a vision, articulating company values and missions cannot be developed solely by adherence to a system. An empowerment style of leadership cannot be conveyed and practised by adherence to checklists.

## Company cultures cannot be created by adherence to a checklist

Management style has to be agreed and driven by those who manage the business. This can take place only if managers are self-critical about their own performance. Change in behaviour has to come from the top. It is not a case of pass the parcel; the senior team must have the passion to succeed. If companies want change, they must work with people who understand the dynamics of how employees can work together. If companies require a change in behaviour, employing consultants with a focus on O&M and procedural change will not produce the results required.

## Summary and Bullet Points

I have highlighted the importance of changing not just a small part of the sub system of the organisation but the very fabric of the business. A holistic approach leads to enduring change. The single most important aspect of change is sustainability.

Sustainability is created only when organisations have trained their own internal resource to drive the process of change. It is to this component which organisations should address themselves in the next two years, for without internal capability there are no drivers. And without committed drivers there is no change.

- Either people are for change or against it. There's no sitting on the fence.

- The role of the top team is to sell the process of change.

- Work with the optimists.

- Convince the pessimists, highlighting specific benefits to the business and personal benefits from change.

- People are not influenced by managers selling features of a programme or a sequence of activities. They buy in to the benefits and what's in it for them.

- Sell the benefits.

- Drive the need for continual change .

- Develop a threat and opportunity matrix highlighting why we need to change in the short and long term. Understand that there are compelling reasons to make improvements.

- Self assess past change initiatives and examine why they failed.

- A main cause for failure of change programmes is lack of tangible implementation and sustainability.

- Consider the time, energy, optimism, aspirations and enthusiasm that is wasted when you don't commit to implementation.

- Focus upon implementation rather than theory.

- Systems and protocols are important. But they never create strong values and passion for customers.

- A culture is shaped by values and behaviours, not protocols and processes.

*Chapter 4:*

# Why 90% of Cultural Interventions fail

**When changing cultures, there is often confusion between theory and implementation. 'Theory of familiarity' managers often confuse knowledge of a concept with application of the idea.**

Several years ago, when leading a senior team through a focus session, I really came to understand the term 'familiarity breeds contempt'. We were talking about the way in which the business leaders had identified key areas for improvement in corporate culture. In particular, this group focused upon changing from a fear-driven, punitive, negative sales culture to one of customer focus, empowerment and achievement.

Managerial behaviours which supported the old culture were identified and discouraged. Many positive, new behaviours were being demonstrated. Several middle managers were making headway, leading briefing sessions and initiating 360 degree appraisals. This was a radical change from six months earlier when appraisals had been imposed from above and only few were valued. Many staff were experimenting with peer review; several had moved into upward appraisal; other challenging souls had adopted a 360 degree view.

## Attention span

We were discussing the merits of this approach, the time needed to adapt and the fact that change for one person can occur in 'a heartbeat' whereas for others it can be a lengthy, painful, but nonetheless productive process. It was at this stage that one of the group interrupted his colleagues: "We've heard all this before — can't we move on to something new?"

## Negative belief : been there, seen it!

I stopped to listen and came to the conclusion that this statement hid a negative belief which should be confronted and challenged. Although many senior officers have been there and seen it, they certainly have not done it.

Furthermore, this is a major issue of which not too many management teams are aware. Discussion around a subject can create a belief that words equate to action. But discussion of a subject does not guarantee that words are reflected in deeds. In some businesses, managers think that because they talk the language, then change is automatically happening. Nothing could be further from the truth.

## Fantastic theory – lousy implementation

The case above is characteristic of many where the consultant has a special role to play with the client – that of the keeper of the corporate conscience. This means ensuring words are reflected in actions. It means working with the senior management to ensure change takes place, that change starts with taking decisive action.

Without action, there is no change. This is especially evident in the UK and the US, where analytical capabilities are overvalued and form the basis for judgements to stop, rather than start, doing things. Far more time and attention is spent on critically assessing the downside of a proposal, and its relative risk, than on making things happen.

To develop a healthy organisation requires a degree of stretch into the discomfort zone. We need cultures where risk aversion is challenged and where action replaces analysis paralysis. This should help replace teams of managers who analyse 101 reasons why something will not work, rather than putting into action what will work. Familiarity with, and application of, a concept do not inevitably equate to implementation.

It is better to focus on behavioural outcomes and implementation than on theory. Culture change is a practical science based upon a theory of action. We should be projecting massive action – not thrusting ourselves into volumes of academic texts.

## Finding 101 ways to make an idea fail!

This is best represented by reference to a case study relating to a change in corporate culture within a financial services company. I had been speaking about the importance of leadership in the process of change and suggested we really should employ 100% of a person – their aspirations, hopes and motivation.

I also suggested we should find out more about staff. For instance, what did they do outside working hours? Did they have a partner? Children? What motivated and interested them in and outside work hours?

The larger part of the group, about 60%, were keen to find out what motivated staff. The remainder, feeling that this was an intrusion into privacy, did little. They were uncomfortable with the process of finding out just what drove their people.

Two weeks later, the large group met again. Those willing to share the results of their investigations concluded that:

- Staff have many social and psychological motives for work. The key drivers were identified as recognition (not reward) and being valued as part of a team.

- If staff felt undervalued, they were more likely to pursue outside interests to help meet unsatisfied needs. For instance, staff at very low grades often pursued responsible positions within voluntary sector organisations or in golf, bowling, dance, community and drama groups.

- Staff had many personal motivations and were far more complex to understand when managers took more than a passive, passing interest in them.

Managers (who did not support this view) were clearly surprised. They said their reason for non-completion of the exercise was the perceived invasion of privacy of staff. The real reason was their inability to experiment, try new (if uncomfortable) behaviours and become real man managers. They further stated, defensively, that most people come to work for purely financial rewards; all they were interested in was pay and promotion.

There was clearly an issue of perception. Those managers who opposed involvement with staff found 101 reasons to make a good idea fail — but couldn't find one good reason to make it work.

## What to do: turning familiarity around

Clearly, we operate in an environment in which another quick fix is always coming. We need to stick to the knitting and make present strategies work. We should stop seeking the quick fix. There is no one solution for the problems we face. However, to make any change effective, and to make any change stick, we must adopt a more positive approach to change. This requires sustainability. To be sustainable, the approach should be simple to understand. But even more important, people have to know where they fit in and the role they should play.

## Knowing is not enough – massive action is critical

Success, whether personal or corporate, is based upon expending massive amounts of energy to create change. We need to adopt a bias for action and assess progress at regular intervals. This means talking about what didn't work and rethinking, redesigning to ensure it does.

## Analogy of learning to walk and mastering change

Think of a child first learning to walk. He may stand up clutching the side of a chair, attempt to walk, and fall. Again, he may stand, take a step and falter. Interestingly, he keeps on trying – knowing that he will walk. But as you watch the child, do you think "Well, he's fallen over twice. It looks as though he's not going to walk." Of course not, because that is a negative belief. You believe the child will walk when he has practised enough. If this were the case, none of us would walk, swim or do the incredible things that humans do. We persevere, time and time again. This is equally true within organisations. This analogy is exactly the same when experimenting and taking risks in business. It is not confined to personal skills but relates well to persistence in organisational change. In similar fashion, the following anecdote illustrates the outcome of an amazing investment in self-belief and time. I wonder whether this could be true in an organisational context.

## Colonel Sanders and success

The well known story behind Colonel Sanders' Kentucky Fried Chicken road to fame started after he had retired at the age of 65. He recognised that all he had was a simple recipe which could be sold to restaurant owners. He believed that, in return, he would receive a small commission which would eventually make him a wealthy man. The recipe was his only resource.

He failed to sell his fried chicken recipe to 1,008 Restaurants. After all, restaurant owners already have a recipe for fried chicken. Eventually, he developed a huge, world-wide franchise – which would never have worked if the Law of Familiarity had not been turned on its head. Now relate this to organisation change. How often have you heard "re-engineering/Total Quality/culture change will never work here" or "that idea would never be implemented". We need to look for a better way.

## If you don't make time to plan, you plan to fail

Ideas are often implemented badly because people fail to think through key issues and consider the scope and impact of implementation. In reality, most ideas could be implemented if planning time was invested. If we plan thoroughly, we prevent problems arising.

There is no law of certainty that the same idea will work to the same degree in different organisations. Similar strategies applied in two companies providing the same service and working in the same industrial sector, may have different results — simply because of the failure to plan in context. Behaviour and how people react, can be predicted if time is devoted to the purpose.

## Hands on change

The approach to change has to be hands on. If we want to create change we have to be part of the process; we cannot distance ourselves from it. This is why so many change initiatives fail. Those who should be driving the change pass the parcel to others. This cascading process of downgrading the responsibility for implementation to the lowest level sends an important signal to everyone in the business: 'this change initiative isn't important'.

## The law of repetition

The key to implementation is repetition. Think of your personal life. If you had not learned about the synchronised use of a clutch and gearbox, you would never have driven a car. If you had failed to practise your diction of French verbs, you would never have learned to speak French. If you had failed to practise effective communication, you would never have developed managerial skills.

Repetition is the key to success. Learning to practise, to improve, to be self-critical, and seek feedback from others is key to personal improvement. So why, when we change the context from personal learning to organisational learning or change, do we adopt a different viewpoint? Unless change is instantaneous, we say the 'theory does not hold water', rather than trying again and again, using different routes to implementation.

If the benefits sought are not apparent almost overnight, the change initiative is deemed to have failed. Apply this reasoning to learning to play golf, dance or swim and it lacks credibility. We expect too much from minimal effort.

The law of repetition is based on closing the loop through continuous feedback by taking action and learning, taking action and learning, and so on. Relating this to organisational change requires these actions:

• Never set impossible targets for culture change. Throw the esoteric stuff out of the window.

• Drive three areas for improvement until they give you the return you want. When it is realised the management group is not going to stop investing massive action into a project until the objectives are achieved, you will see a higher level of commitment from middle managers and others.

• Never give a managerial group responsibility for critical objectives because ownership will never reside with an individual – it will reside with a group. Make individuals responsible and relentlessly request feedback on progress. Don't show interest in why things don't work. Measure performance on what each individual makes work.

• Make it a rule never to say "it won't work." For every negative comment you receive ask for two ways to make 'it' work .

• Things only work with the support of people. If they don't work, perhaps you need to communicate more effectively. It may be that you have chosen the wrong person as the change agent.

## Specific issues which can lead to failure

When planning any form of culture change, attention should be focused on specific areas. Understanding the culture of the business, and building a strong mission driven by core values which guide behaviour are obvious. But the following points are worth considering, since research highlights tangible reasons why major change initiatives fail.

Monitoring and assessing progress is critical. Most change initiatives focused on quality and customer orientation have several driving features. In this context I focus on four key areas in which education and skill development, reflected in action, must be progressed.

## 1  Measuring improvement and failure

## 2  Internal teamwork

## 3  Change management

## 4  Preventative action and planning

The most common problems to be addressed are:

## 1  Measuring improvement and failure

Generally it is accepted that, in order to promote improvement, you need to measure performance. Because poor performance is often difficult to measure, and exists between internal silos of the business, it is necessary to focus on performance failures. This is relatively easy in a manufacturing business, in which defects stick out like a sore thumb, but as you move into the service sector failure becomes less easy to identify.

It is important to measure wasted effort – a lost opportunity which has been resourced at some time. We refer to this as reworking a job, the 'cost of errors.' In the service industry, over 40% of salary costs are wasted in fixing things after they have gone wrong.

A major theme then in a customer-focused business is to measure and equate a cost to problems. Some people refer to this as cost of quality, a central theme in most improvement programmes. Here are some of the problems associated with poor implementation:

### Pre-occupation with measuring only tangible activities can lead to customer service failure

Often the only measures generated are in the hard, tangible manufacturing areas. Rework and failure costs must be measured in frequently neglected service and administrative areas. In one organisation, an insurance business, we helped managers identify more than 300 work activities which were classed as rework. These activities consumed time but added little value to the business because they should have been performed right first time.

## Communicating the impact on failure of the performance of the business

If staff are going to the trouble to record figures which reflect failure, it makes sense to display these figures to let others know 'how we are doing'. All too often, information on rework is hidden away in filing cabinets and on computer discs. The phrase, 'what gets measured and is communicated, gets done' is an important guide.

### Expect instant results

The diagram on the next page (Diagram 3) has helped to sell culture change. It works on the basis that we expend time on four key activities: we add value; we rework things when they go wrong; we inspect for accuracy; and we prevent problems arising. The ratio of costs in the 'poor quality' business is completely distorted by firefighting culture with a heavy emphasis on rework. When changing the culture, we focus on devoting substantial resource to prevention. This investment will reduce the need to check things, thereby reducing rework costs. But change does not always happen overnight. Initially, the organisation has to over invest in prevention to get rid of the rework culture. This is best represented by the formula 10P(prevention) = 1R(rework). Initially, to kick in real change requires ten units of prevention to eliminate one unit of rework. We demand such an investment because the power of the firefighting culture is so strong that there is need for an initial momentum and a strong drive to launch the change. As the diagram shows, the shift in emphasis but does not detail the cultural changes which have to be implemented. Managers may expect instant results from an intervention – which is not always the case. Many practitioners of change know this is true but use the diagram to sell the idea of instant results.

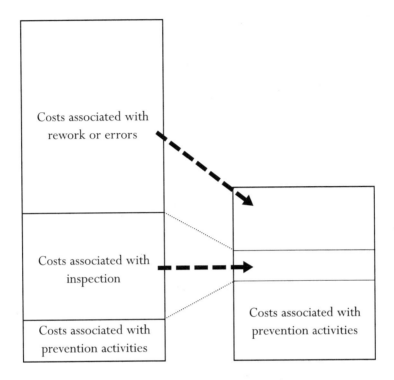

*Diagram 3. Cost of errors: before and after culture change*

## 2   Internal teamwork

The easiest way to discover whether an organisation is working effectively is to examine the relationships between functions, departments and locations. A key focus of culture change should be to 'knock down the walls'. Note the variety of cultures which exist within a medium to large scale company. The culture of one department may be radically different to that of others. A major shift should be made to generate positive working relationships between functions, ensuring everybody is pulling in the same direction.

It is critical that functions and departments which depend on each other see each other as a part of continuous process – a supply chain with seamless service. In reality, however, too many organisations develop cultures based on functional expertise; they often work in spite of each other.

## Sub optimal strategy

It is remarkable how often strategies owned by functional areas within a large organisation are unknown to other areas. If this is not challenged, it can create win/lose relationships and a climate of low mutual trust. This is indicated by the success of the corporate grapevine and the negative outcomes of pointless political battles which take place.

## Prefer ambiguity

We have witnessed situations in which key business drivers heading functions prefer to "keep their options open". They purposely create a climate of ambiguity where staff do not know what is expected of them. This translates into failing to set objectives and provide information to others.

Difficulties associated with change have been traced mostly to departmental heads running their own empire without consideration, concern or care for the business as a whole. The sooner these people are encouraged to leave, the sooner simplicity can reign and staff be allowed to get on with their jobs. The watchword should be "if at first you can't change the people, change the people".

## 3    Change management

## Attitude – who me?

Change can be effective only when we lead by example, but the common theme in some companies is still 'it's his fault not mine'. This is characteristic of a blame culture where the guilty are hunted, then publicly humiliated. This fear culture (and it is common) has to be broken. Changing the white knuckle response of senior managers whose first reaction is "whose fault is it?", to "that's unfortunate, how can we ensure it never happens again?" is very difficult to inculcate. But it is central to those lower in the hierarchy who may be reluctant to open up and discuss major problems between departments.

## Lack of critical ability – looking in the mirror

A reflection of the paragraph above is the unfortunate tendency for managers looking for ways to improve personal effectiveness. Again, in a fearful climate there are no rewards for admitting a lack of competence. This is where the philosophy of the learning organisation is undersold or not understood. Continual learning and a self-critical attitude are especially important with regard to promoting a philosophy of continuous improvement.

## Firefighting culture

Far too many businesses have a strong fire-fighting philosophy. In terms of the planning cycle, too little time is devoted to planning and integration of projects and too much to the school of "Ready, Aim, Fire " management. This lack of discipline and control leads to a chaotic environment in which everyone is busy but less-than-optimum value is added.

## Never enough time

Perhaps the biggest killer of culture change is the well-quoted, "We do not have enough time." If this response fails, the other is half-whispered, "Listen, I know it's important but I get judged on what we ship – that's what I get paid for and that's what I'll do." This 'Its more than my job's worth' syndrome sends sharp signals to everybody else within the company. Once this virus spreads, a management exhortation on commitment is the only way out.

# 4   Preventative action and planning

## Unfreeze departmental attitudes

Unfreezing some attitudes, promoting team effectiveness and win/win relationships is a major behavioural intervention and one which is often avoided. The traditional war games exist between the sales function and admin. support. In a financial services company the admin support people did as much as they could to alienate the external customer through bureaucracy and by putting up road blocks. No one thought to tell them that the customer paid their wages. Staff in some areas are so far removed from the customer they have lost all 'customer focus' and are no more than paper pushers. They are not to blame, but those who manage them have to tune in to the customer revolution. Similarly, line management in many companies do not see or share the same goals; their relationship is less than optimum.

## Over the wall

A failure to take personal responsibility for change needs to be remedied. In the same company, a divisional general manager received a phone call from an irate customer and made every effort to resolve the problem himself. The grateful customer will continue to do business with the company .Why? The general manager's response was so uncharacteristic that the customer was impressed.

## Training is a waste of time

Change does not come about in neat packages. Even planned change is erratic, difficult and painful, which means it can also be time-consuming. Failure to invest in prevention (ie training), can kill a drive. Line managers who make life difficult for staff attending training workshops do not realise that every action they take supports the view that the organisation is not serious about culture change.

## Quick fix: If it ain't broke, don't mend it

The reputation for the quick fix is still prevalent. Too often there is a failure to prioritise and no sense of urgency for any task which does not have to be completed that day.

## Not wanting change

The real problem for Total Quality and culture change is people who do not want to change, or who believe that change will stop and they can get back to normal. If change is not painful, it is not working. We all need to be involved in the process. If a fire-fighting culture is allowed to remain, there will be nothing but cosmetic change.

## Summary and bullet points

Changing culture never has been easy. Too many management groups focus on what is wrong with their present strategy, rather than working on implementation of change. There are literally thousands of ways of introducing culture change. Some take longer, others are bottom up – some are systems-driven, others rely on trust and empowerment. Committed and massive action has to be expended to fight the 'familiarity' syndrome. What we have seen before does not equate to what we have done before.

- A change in mindset is critical to change within most organisations. This is a fundamental problem which has halted many initiatives in the last ten years.

- Repetition is a process which every athlete, student, manager or parent believes in to improve personal skills. It is the first positive step when changing theory into action. . . and success.

- Senior teams need to commit to action, not confuse words with deeds

- Familiarity with a concept does not always equate to implementation of the concept.

- You only truly understand a subject when you can teach it. This may be a useful driver for senior people who could become key change agents.

- Don't look for 101 ways to make a good idea fail. Look for one to make it work.

- Knowing a subject is not enough. Success comes from committing to massive degrees of action.

- Try until you succeed – remember the Kentucky Fried Chicken experience.

- Change should always be an active 'hands on' process.

# Chapter 5 :

# Understanding Corporate Culture

To shape corporate culture for enhanced business performance we need to understand the key determinants and the action which can be taken.

Culture in many companies evolves slowly and is blown along by events and key actors, more often by accident than by design. In order to create a strong culture, it is important to understand the dynamics of culture change. This was partially achieved in Chapter 2 when we used the 9 S's framework and is the foundation which we will build upon now.

## The cultural iceberg

Like an iceberg, the culture of a business is largely submerged. There are few places in any business where the culture is directly observable. And to take the iceberg analogy further, the deeper we go the more difficult it is to identify tangible elements of the culture. But even though there is difficulty in defining and feeling, seeing and touching the culture, we still recognise that it is real and vibrant. It will have a major impact on the performance of the business, even though some of the key drivers of the culture are less obvious to observers. An organisation will consciously display symbols or communicate certain messages which depict its culture. Note also that many aspects of the culture operate at an 'other than conscious' level. Much about the organisation, operating well below the surface, requires extensive research to fully understand the true dynamics to bring about change.

## Unconscious presence

We operate at a conscious and unconscious level. Many of our personal desires, motivations and behaviours are driven by our unconscious or subconscious mind - that aspect of our mind which is 'other than conscious'. In a similar fashion, there are aspects of corporate culture which operate at the unconscious level and are very powerful in shaping behaviour. In human beings, many of our physical and mental processes are driven by our 'other than conscious' processes. For instance, breathing or running are not conscious activities. If we had to work out consciously all the actions necessary to run for a bus we would spend an inordinate amount of time planning the run. Likewise, if we had to breathe consciously all the time we would never be able to do anything more complex. And as many of the ways in which we behave are shaped by 'other than conscious' processes, organisations are driven in a similar way.

## What is it about culture that can shape events?

It is difficult to establish what it is about the culture that produces a specific instance, outcome or event. Only by studying the major causes of culture are we able to understand the action we can take to shape events. All we can be certain of is that an organisational culture has an unconscious presence which is extremely powerful; the value of understanding its composition can help us to improve performance. Later we will explain the key determinants of corporate culture and the action we can take to build a strong culture.

## One culture or many?

Interestingly, any company can have a dominant culture as well as many cultures. And multiple cultures will be driven by specific circumstances. It is clear that many factors shape the culture. Our journey is to find out more about what managers can do to create a culture which suits their purpose.

## Culture: good or bad; positive or negative; strong or weak?

Business cultures, good or bad, can be categorised along a number of dimensions. Some cultures are strong and forceful but there is no promise that they create wonderful atmospheres for people to work. I have experienced very powerful dominant and strong cultures which are also categorised as negative, punitive and fear driven - not great places to work. Although some aspects of the culture may be favourable, not all aspects may be viewed in the same positive light. It is important to understand that a weak culture may not be all bad - its relative weakness may enable positive managers and staff to influence events based upon their perception of what is right or wrong. Given that desirable personal values can shape a weak culture, a dictatorial and insecure manager can soon create a dominant climate which is geared solely to meet his needs. Culture change is a complex issue and one which can be addressed on a number of levels.

## So what shapes corporate culture?

When a business is created, the founders or owners are its architects, carefully crafting the mission of the organisation to meet its objectives. The views, personal values and passions of the businessman are often evident in 'how things are organised'. Such organisation can become the dominant or norm of 'acceptable behaviour' for dealing with issues and key constituents within the business. As the organisation grows, key individuals shape events. People, senior managers, key players, intervene and their motives and behaviours become evident in the day-to-day behaviour of how things are done. If these behaviours are repeated, sooner or later they become ingrained habits for how issues are normally dealt with. In some cases, the behaviours are translated and absorbed into organisational systems, processes and protocols. In other words, behaviours and actions of influential actors in the company shape the way in which the company deals with issues.

Dependent upon whether actions and behaviours are positive or negative, company practices are perceived as good or bad. Conflicts arise when key players have different rules or values in how they organise things. At this critical stage, the culture is shaped by consciously agreeing on 'what is important' and 'what is not'. If there is a failure to understand that consistency is required, and if key players fail to agree on 'how to do business', different cultures will emerge within the company.

For instance, the finance department may display strong control and regulatory culture where attention to detail and conformity to protocols and systems are applied rigorously. In the same company, on the same floor, marketing executives value taking risks in a volatile market. Sales people are focused entirely on generating revenue by promising more than the production people can deliver; all they concern themselves with is 'closing the sale'. Is it any surprise there are major conflicts? Each part of the business has different 'values' and operates in spite of the other. We can deduce from this example that there will be a strong mis-alignment resulting in poor levels of quality and customer service.

These problems are evident because the key actors, individual managers, have formed their part of the business on the basis of personal values. This mis-alignment, occurring by accident - not by design - needs to be thrashed out at senior levels. The action agreed should be communicated throughout the business.

That is what happens in most organisations. A variety of cultures, or sub cultures, exist - each driven by the values of key managers. As managers move on and new managers take over, restructure aspects of business cultures evolve and change. But they are never shaped purposely to meet the real demands of the business.

## Role of technology

Technology can shape business culture. For instance, in organisations driven by continuous processes, such as chemicals, plastics and petroleum, technology will shape organisational structure and the way things are organised. The scope of jobs may largely determine how work is organised and the very nature of work will determine relationships between people who manage and work the process. With continuous flow technology, there is often a need for strict division of labour, with specialisation a key driver keeping costs low. But beware. Social costs in this environment can be high through lack of scope for individual attainment, developing amiable working relationships and strong group working.

**You can develop a highly-empowered culture driven by self-managed groups and still be the lowest cost producer in the industry. You have to work at it. But it won't happen by accident.**

However, in continuous flow technology there is scope to re-engineer relationships so that economies of large scale production are still evident, with cross-functional working and overlapping relationships at all levels. Case studies in continuous flow technology industries have shown how hierarchical levels of management can be replaced by self-managed teams. These teams take on responsibility for organising themselves to fulfil requirements of the task.

## White collar continuous process

In the 'white collar' environment, people in many processes are organised on a continuous process flow. For instance, many banks and financial institutions have been driven by a strong desire to rationalise processes to ensure consistency and group people into strict divisions of labour. Information technology has created continuous processes in which resultant working relationships have a direct impact on the culture. Moving away from rigid division of labour, and strict functional management to re-engineering processes around the customer will impact significantly upon the culture. For instance, I have worked with an insurance business to enable its culture to change radically from a 'strong dependent' culture where employees were told 'what to do' and 'when to do it'. In the new culture 'cross functional working' and constant innovation with a strong customer focus was to become the norm.

The technology employed will shape the business culture. Where technology dictates how work is processed, there will be a requirement to conform. Where technology does not have such a stranglehold, there is more scope for flexibility – and more room for confusion and ambiguity.

It is generally agreed that technology can determine the culture. A business can be shaped to conform to meet cost requirements, but this does not mean it cannot meet with other more human requirements.

Perhaps it is time that you applied these concepts to your own organisation. Think through some of the following issues.

## Cultural issues

• When communicating outside the company, upon what does your organisation focus most attention?

• When communicating with staff and customers, what aspects of the organisation appear strong and which appear weak?

- How would you describe your organisation? Does it resemble a tiger or a dinosaur?

- What words best describe how you do business? How would others, in different functions, define the business?

- What type of staff behaviour does the organisation encourage?

- On the following dimensions, how would you describe your culture?

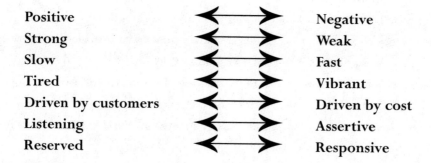

| | | |
|---|---|---|
| Positive | | Negative |
| Strong | | Weak |
| Slow | | Fast |
| Tired | | Vibrant |
| Driven by customers | | Driven by cost |
| Listening | | Assertive |
| Reserved | | Responsive |

On what dimension would others, who occupy key positions in the business, place your organisation? And, using these categories, how would staff and customers appraise the business?

## Summary and bullet points

This introduction to corporate culture suggested that, because of its lack of substance and tangibility, much of it is difficult to define. Much of the behaviour within a company is driven by 'other' than 'conscious' forces which at first are not too apparent. The iceberg analogy is useful because it suggests the deeper we go in understanding the culture, the wider the base becomes. As we progress through this text, we will identify the real drivers, but we need to address important issues before we move on to detail.

- Cultures exist by design or by accident.

- You cannot not have a culture.

- Many apparent unconscious forces shape the culture.

- You can have a powerful and strong culture and climate yet still find negative elements. Note the highly powered business driven by fear.

- Weak cultures can become easily moulded by key people.

- Cultures are shaped by people - by their values, thoughts, beliefs and actions.

- Once you start to understand the determinants of culture, you can define it. If you can define it, you can measure change. And if you can measure changes in the culture, you can shape it.

- Look at the dominant factors which shape your business, then compare your views with colleagues.

- What do your customers pick up most about your culture?

*Chapter 6 :*

# The Cultural Iceberg

In the next few chapters we will examine the way in which cultures can be shaped and driven to new forms. But first it is important to develop the core model which will help us understand the dominant drivers behind culture. For the sake of simplicity, we can see the iceberg (Diagram 4) as six levels of factors representing cause effect relationships. Each factor will, in turn, influence other factors within the culture.

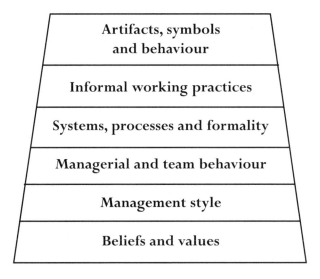

*Diagram 4. The cultural iceberg*

The core model is reflected in six levels. Starting from the base, 'beliefs and values' shape the culture of the business. Beliefs include 'shared beliefs' held by the core drivers. Beliefs, like values, are never right or wrong; they are just beliefs — of what is important and not important to an individual. Beliefs:

• Indicate what is important to oneself

• Highlight a higher moral understanding of how to behave

• Tell us how a person perceives the world

• Will shape actual behaviour

We can argue at length about the merits of beliefs that each of us hold, but beliefs can neither be proven nor disproven as right or wrong. They simply reflect the moral code and experience of a person, or group of people. We hear elders say that people no longer have values these days. This is untrue. More accurately, values that others hold are alien to them; or values do not reflect ideas of what is right and wrong.

Beliefs help us shape our values. If our beliefs change, we will see a consequent shift in what we value. So the two are interwoven. This is true on a personal as well as organisational level.

If we spend time talking with a top team, elicit their shared beliefs and test them for understanding, we will be in a strong position to predict the behaviour of this team. In this example, let's look at five beliefs owned by two different teams.

One team listed their beliefs as:

• Customer focused

• Team driven

• Personal development

- Commercial success

- Achievement

  Another team listed their beliefs as:

- Driven by profit

- Cost reduction as a tool of continuous improvement

- Setting goals and objectives

- Strict lines of command

- Loyalty

When confronted with choices of how top teams will respond as business leaders, you will find that these two teams will react very differently. What is important and valued highly by one team appears completely alien to the other. One 'belief' system is not right, and the other wrong. They are just different and indicate that behaviour is guided by what business leaders hold dear. All actions and behaviour are guided by beliefs. This is evident when we see how history has unfolded and note how dominant characters shape events. They are driven by their beliefs. This characteristic is shared from the President of the United States to the chief executive of Ford, to the leader of a major trade union, to the middle manager of any company or public organisation. Understand beliefs and values before analysing behaviour.

## How beliefs shape management style

Beliefs held by a manager will influence the way he manages. Many years ago Douglas McGregor developed an interesting view on management style. His research, still extremely relevant, suggested the assumptions or beliefs which a manager has on the 'nature of man' will shape the way he manages people. According to McGregor's simple model, the manager assumed that:

• Work is inherently distasteful to most people.

• Most people have little interest in work, are not ambitious, have little desire for responsibility and prefer to be directed.

• Most people have to be coerced, rewarded or punished before their commitment to organisational goals is gained.

• Most people have little interest in, or capability for, contributing towards the solution of organisational problems.

• People are motivated only by reward and punishment.

• Most people require constant control and are often threatened with sanctions to achieve organisational objectives.

These fundamental beliefs about man, which McGregor referred to as Theory X Style, would create a dictatorial or highly controlling style of management.

Alternatively, a manager may have these assumptions about human nature:

• Work is pleasant and as natural as play, if the conditions are favourable.

• Workers have discipline and self control to achieve organisational objectives.

• Workers are motivated by things other than reward or sanctions.

• The capability for contributing to the wider enterprise is dispersed throughout the workforce.

- People are motivated by things other than money. Self esteem, recognition, group belonging are psychological factors.

- It is natural for people to be self directed and creative at work, provided the conditions allow.

Management style should be modified to enable individuals to be valued for their willing contribution, participation and consultation. This McGregor referred to as Theory X style of management

Because leadership has come a long way, it is unfashionable to quote McGregor. I disagree with this perspective because modern theorists on leadership and management style have spent little time exploring the 'nature of man'. Only when managers understand the importance of values and beliefs, will they be able to understand the complexities of organisational culture and, more importantly, how to change it for the better. Without analysis of dominant management style there will be little move forward, merely a tinkering and tweaking at the surface.

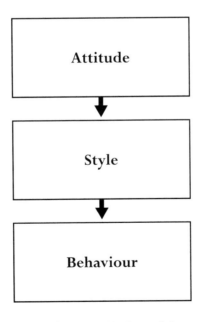

*Diagram 5. Style fundamentally changes behaviour*

## People are boss watchers

Attitude and style have a deep influence on managerial and team behaviour. A strong style of management can add direction and alignment to an organisation, whereas a weak or indifferent style creates confusion and lack of clarity. Again, an over-dominant, forceful style needs to be refocused on listening for suggestions for improvements and developing people as team players. Ideas come along very quietly. Managers need to be aware that people are 'boss watchers', always assessing and testing whether what the boss says is a true reflection of how he or she behaves.

### 'Nothing changes until behaviour changes'

This statement has driven me to understand the dynamics of social interaction and to search for as many ways as possible to understand how to improve communication and influence people in organisations. A belief which guides my behaviour is *'we should create change through influence rather than control'*. This belief has shaped my behaviour to believe the message 'what people receive from me is the message I have sent'. The onus is on me to ensure that what I send is thoroughly tested and not ambiguous. This is even more important when we are confronted with the less-than-positive person to whom change is a major challenge. So however negative a person's perception of a problem on organisational change, I always seek and find a new way to influence and persuade, be willing to persist and revisit old ground, question assumptions, ask questions and listen. By focusing upon the 'persuasion paradigm' we can learn as well as influence. When we are listening we have greater scope to hear what is important to an individual — his or her values.

## How is behaviour shaped?

If we have a broadly consistent style of management, certain norms will be created within the organisation. These norms will become the expected standards of behaviour. This begins to break down when there is a misalignment of styles or where styles exist, evolve and develop by accident. This is very much the default style of management where individual styles, based upon past experience only and without guidance, are applied.

We are all aware of managers who manage by staying within their comfort zone. They are absorbed in the technical nature of their job and do not attempt to influence events. This is the challenge for many companies — to move towards developing a variety of effective management styles which are applied with ease and when circumstances demand. This implies that management styles and leadership can be learned. Central to any cultural change initiative is the devoting of resources to train people who manage people.

If style is a prime determinant of behaviour, how can we be sure we are inculcating the right sort or variety of behaviour? We need to know and agree set standards of performance including:

- Interacting with others

- Meeting management

- Training staff

- Motivating teams

- Joint objective setting

- Decision making

- Problem solving

- Undertaking briefing meetings

- Leading groups

This can be easily achieved by listening to the answers to these two questions:

**What do we need to do more of. . .?**

**What do we need to do less of. . .?**

Listening, and agreeing performance standards is central to effective culture change. It is, too, central to setting up the next level within the culture: that of systems, processes and protocols, which are, in effect, the formal methods by which an organisation transacts business with itself, then transacts business with its external customers.

## Failure to develop systems

Form follows action. Without action there is no process, so the behaviours which people display provide guidance on developing standards. These standards can help formally outline how we transact business with others, whether internal or external customers and suppliers. In many cases, systems and the codification of formal processes evolve from specified needs and how people evolve work patterns. The formal system so created should facilitate speedy and consistent transaction of business when it evolves around business needs. But if the formal system becomes an end in itself there can be confusion. Take, for example, the drive to achieve set standards such as ISO accreditation. A whole industry has mushroomed devoted to providing organisations with a documented system stating process flows regarding the way the organisation transacts business. This guided documentation will clarify roles, responsibilities and the flow of services but it is no substitute for cultural evaluation and change.

The benefits of documenting processes are considerable but when they are perceived as being more important than investing in generating the core business, they are no more than a quick fix.

As we move towards the top of the iceberg we see more of the culture. And much of it becomes tangible. The next level is the informal way of working. It is best typified by the climate which keeps people at the office and gets them into work early to adjust and compensate for that which the system cannot achieve. The informal organisation is basically the total of informal agreements and the atmosphere which people create to facilitate closure on processes. The systems may not have catalogued all the part numbers but a member of staff from inventory will be able to recall that which the system has neglected. The finance officer, who regularly stays late at the end of the month to double check invoices and credit notes, typifies the commitment unmeasured but essential to the success of any business.

The informal system or organisation compensates for that which the formal system neglects. The informal organisation makes things tick and people take personal responsibility to go beyond the specificity of their job role or description. The health of an organisation, often discernible at the level of the informal organisation, is easily measured for it includes the motivations, morale and climate of the business. Just being exposed to the informal organisation will often tell the careful researcher more about the culture than owners or senior managers are aware. By talking with people, either on a one-to-one basis or in focus groups, the perceptive student of organisational culture can develop hypotheses about how things are and how they can be improved. He will focus upon the cause effect relationships that need to be assessed.

On the surface of the cultural iceberg we may witness the artefacts and symbols that separate what is important from that which is not. Examine the layout of the office, how you are greeted when you make contact with the organisation either in person or on the phone, staff restaurant layout, how people talk to you, allocation of car parking spaces, tidiness, how issues on confidentiality are addressed, and criteria for selection and advancement. All these factors highlight the most obvious aspects of the organisation. To gain a fuller understanding of this level of analysis we need to understand how the organisation chooses to communicate with its core constituents — its customers, staff and shareholders. Consistency and clarity are vital, illustrating how successful the business is in influencing key players in the marketplace.

## Summary and bullet points

I have examined the dynamics of the cultural iceberg and will go into greater depth in the following chapters. But it must be remembered that the core beliefs and values of the business will shape and determine the culture more than anything else.

An organisation cannot <u>not</u> have a culture. However, the top team can choose how it will be shaped.

- Beliefs of the owners or founders will initially shape its direction and mission.

- As an organisation evolves, the culture will change, Either it can be directed or it will evolve through chance and circumstance.

- Technology will impact upon organisational structures, people and therefore the culture. Examine cause effect relationships if you are heavily dependent upon technology for determining process flows.

- Culture change should be a deliberate process with clear ideas on specific aspects to change and improve.

- Some attempt must be made to categorise the culture. Use the 9 S's or the categories in the main body of the text.

- Management style is critical in shaping behaviour.

- All staff are boss watchers and look for match or synchronisation with what you say with your deeds.

- Nothing changes until behaviour changes. This should be modelled by managers.

- Over-compensation of systems, process mapping and protocols will never compensate for an enduring focus on deliberate and planned culture change.

- The informal organisation, a good indicator of the health of the organisation, should gel with formal structures and systems.

- The informal organisation should complement the formal and not compensate for inadequate or inappropriate controls and protocols.

- The most visible part of the culture probably highlights what needs to be looked at in the business at a much deeper level. Analysis at this level should generate the right questions to ask.

*Chapter 7:*

# Vision, Mission, Values, Strategic Planning

## The Strategy

There are compelling arguments in favour of developing a strong vision, mission and set of values. It will come as no surprise that a result of conducting a rigorous cultural survey is usually a major enquiry into clarifying the strategic direction of the company.

Put bluntly, the disadvantages of not having a firm direction in terms of values and mission can be significant. For instance, the culture of the business will exist but may not be controlled. When key leaders move on, the culture can actually change for the worse because their presence and influence no longer has a strongly positive effect. Charismatic Leaders who move on leave a vacuum which cannot always be filled. These people can instigate an inspiring climate for others to develop.

For some organisations the culture is maintained but never led or driven with any force or intensity. The danger with a barely maintained culture is that positive 'role models', which others can emulate, never come to the fore; there can be confusion about what managerial behaviour is acceptable and what is not. This ambiguity may mean that vague performance standards will proliferate and no real leadership will evolve. With vague values and corporate culture emerging, management control will tend to be the focus rather than values of empowerment, teamwork and trust becoming the key vehicles of positive change.

## Advantages of strong values to enhanced business performance

Values are seldom explicitly stated. If they are, they should at least be real and give some intellectual clarity to the purpose of the organisation. Intellectual clarity is the starting point for debate with others on the direction of the business. Many organisations never achieve this degree of rapport with staff. It is essential that the top team and, at least, their direct reports can answer this question.

**What is it we want to do, to have and to become, as an entity?**

The important words here are **do, have** and **become**. This is a critical issue for top team members and the sooner they tackle it, the clearer the vision for the business will become.

Stating the values of the business in clear unambiguous terms, creates an emotional call to staff which results in an emotional commitment and a sense of mission at all levels. It also helps in answering the question 'does the organisation care about what I care about?'

## Outcomes from a cultural review

At this stage of 'value clarification' it is invaluable to conduct an audit of the culture. However this is completed, it must be objective and focused. This enables the correlation of feelings with metrics. It is important that when this is conducted there is a deliberate attempt to triangulate results and to ensure that any quantitative analysis is consistent with qualitative data which may have been collected through focus groups. At this stage there are a number of issues which require clarification before progressing. I have highlighted below some which I have experienced in interventions over many years.

## Managing the response to the cultural review

When giving feedback to the top team, you may not always get the support your require. Recently when working with a large business (the top performing company within their parent's portfolio of businesses) I found the financial director and supporters to be very defensive as to the results of the cultural review. Much of what related to the finance function was less than positive and the financial director had difficulty correlating this with the financial performance of the business. He could not comprehend how the business was expanding their share of the market, and their return on investment, yet cultural factors appeared so bad.

My understanding and the ensuing debate followed a line of questioning:

• What is perceived as being less than positive in the culture?

• Who perceives the issues as important?

• What action has been taken by the top team to test for understanding?

• If there is a misperception, what action can the top team take to address the key issues?

• Why does it take a cultural review, interviews and focus groups to highlight those issues which others perceive is holding the company back?

• Why have these issues not been raised previously with the top team?

The financial director responded positively to the questions. This became a useful method for improving overall perceptions by those at senior levels.

As this cultural review was powerful in helping this company hone performance, with commitment to change being evident, just imagine what they could achieve if they really did develop a high performance culture.

To summarise, what became evident was that the company was 'short term oriented' and their present performance would not continue without some realistic rethinking of strategic direction. Because the parent company was also adopting a value added approach to strategic analysis in all their portfolio companies, our approach gelled well with the wishes of the holding company. Please note, not all are so positive.

## More on culture reviews

Not all top team people react well to a cultural review. It is important to understand that, at top team levels, the sponsor and the agent supporting change has often to manage delicate egos of top team players. So the approach to change management is as important as feeding back the data. Feeding back information in a clinical fashion is of little value. Multiple explanations may be given on the data available and its possible interpretation. The often-quoted response of 'there's the culture review, make of it as you will and take action' is not the sort of consultancy intervention which is geared towards long-term partnering.

If the review has been conducted accurately, you should be able to isolate the response of people in the business by seniority as well as by functional responsibility. Doing this enables quick identification of problems. We use a very detailed series of questionnaires, interviews and focus groups based upon the 9 S's framework (Chapter 2). It is incredibly powerful in helping diagnose problems but the most difficult task is to get the top team to take ownership and commit to action. Some will display a high degree of denial and it is important that the top team sticks with the process. Otherwise the denial will translate into inaction, passive resistance and low commitment to implementing the necessary changes. At this stage, the change agent has to work closely with the top sponsors and not shirk the issues. At the same time he must respect the concerns of those in 'denial'.

## Strategic direction in question

During a cultural review, the information generated is incredibly powerful in helping the company reappraise its position in the market and its future role. I personally like to ensure that clients and sponsors take ownership and recruit the support of their direct reports to action progress. A strong team effort driven by consensus must operate at this level. There must be a seamless interaction between the top team and the next layer down. Simply put, if this is not apparent how will they achieve their goals and how will they communicate within their teams and direct reports? All comments on strategic planning passed in this book focus upon top team and direct reports working closely in unity.

As well as highlighting the need to work on values and beliefs, a cultural review will highlight that the Hard S's, as well as the Soft elements of the 9 S's framework, need to be reworked. In recent times, several companies have found that the direction on which they had focused their energies was not common knowledge with staff. Generally, there was a confusion about the direction the company was taking. Since form follows strategy we were concerned whether the right structure and reporting relationships were in place in order to focus the energies and attention of people to drive towards their goal. This concern resulted in a values and mission clarification exercise, which was very well received.

The same company has now developed a strategic plan to focus upon world markets. It has also conducted a vulnerability analysis of their own business in 40 markets as well as a competitor analysis in each of those markets. The strategic exercise forced sales and technical people to work together on specific issues. Each workshop was driven by 'specificity' meaning, for example, don't think of China as China – isolate the markets, by product, region, risk and maturity. Likewise, think of the former USSR as discrete and separate markets in similar fashion. By so doing, it is possible to develop specific plans to meet specific needs and relative maturity and risk of each market. At the end of this exercise, it was decided that some markets were not worth the associated risk. Accordingly, resources were diverted from what we called the 'dogs' to more promising 'problem children' markets which needed investment.

The company, a major player in the genetics industry, ranked the action necessary to develop its culture for the challenge of 2005. Prior to my involvement with this company, planning was based on predicted sales on three-monthly time scales. They are now conducting a full strategic analysis of the business – all as a result of continued need to re-evaluate the culture. They have turned their culture around. If this is what can be achieved with a successful company, what progress can be made with one barely keeping its head above water?

## The process of creating culture change

The process will be highlighted with reference to a large organisation administering a major service to the public. Located in Scotland, and funded to the tune of £170 million per year, the 300 people who are the organisation have been through a major 'values clarification' exercise which has done much to improve performance. It will be noted how we can strictly move from values to influencing behaviour in what follows.

This organisation is classically public sector in approach except that there had developed a young and innovative top team who were keen to drive change. The CEO and human resources director co-ordinated events and she was keen to appraise performance of their business and relate this to business plans. Part of this drive came from the Government, who were keen to guard the public purse and at the same time ensure that resources were channelled to were they where most needed.

# First steps – mission statement

The top team of any business is not always on the same page and it was imperative that it value and own the process. Sitting together for two days working on mission statements is not going to generate a lot of enthusiasm because many perceive this as no more than setting New Year resolutions. This activity has to be managed and be an inspiring event.

When formulating mission statements, we aim to ensure there is consensus from the top team, that the top team commits to deliberately involve their direct reports and others in the process. It is also critical that they deal with the process with some urgency rather than letting the process limp along without firm direction – (which I have witnessed in too many companies).

When working on a strong mission or values statement, the top team must be visible and reflect its words with action. Perhaps one of the best mission statements I have helped others create took less than 30 minutes. Although not very elegant, 'Beat the Competition!' summed up the company's desperate circumstances at a difficult time. When the company recovered its competitive edge, it could add to its mission statement. But at that time the call brought a sense of urgency: Beat the Competition or close the business! Fancy statements on customer service, quality and teamwork would have done nothing for salesmen who had to get out, negotiate their best deal and deliver to specification at the cost agreed.

**When undertaking a 'values clarification' exercise, the values chosen must reflect the strategy of the business. If not, where is the link between means and ends?**

The direction is the mission; the business strategy explains the steps which depict the commercial process to achieving the mission; and the values should reflect the 'how to's of resource utilisation. In other words, the behaviours and mindsets which will be employed.

One of the best statements is the simply-stated McDonalds Mission: To have a McDonalds restaurant within ten minutes of anyone on the planet. It's powerful and tells us exactly what they intend to do.

## Espoused and real values

We sometimes have a problem ensuring that mission and values become no more than words written on paper. You may have sat in a reception area and read through the values adorned on walls, on plaques on coffee mugs and T-shirts. For instance:

**'In quality we trust'**

**'The customer is King'**

**'Prevention is our creed'**

**'We believe in partnering with our suppliers'**

**'Our staff are our most important asset'**

The above are what I call espoused values – what the company says but does not always deliver. On the occasions where the values are not lived, the cynics among us may interpret these values as:

**'Volume is more important than quality'**

**'Deliver no more to the customer than he is due'**

**'Rework everything, then charge it to the customer'**

**'Pay as little as you can for inputs from suppliers'**

**'Over manage to ensure conformity of behaviour'**

It does not matter what a company's stated values are. The people who work in the organisation know the truth – as do customers and anyone who comes into contact with the company. They can see through the pointless exercise espousing values which will put them at a perceived higher morality. But claiming a higher calling, a superior level of 'service excellence' and communicating this to key constituents is a shabby and futile activity if the basics of service delivery are not met.

---

*Integrity was not a core value*

*I experienced a classic case where the direct reports of a top team were working on value clarification. One of the values chosen for discussion by the top team was 'integrity.' It soon became clear that the direct reports were uncomfortable at going to their customers, and their own teams, claiming a high degree of integrity as a core value of their business. Specifically, several notorious commercial deals had not demonstrated the presence of this value.*
*The top team listened to their reports and agreed to drop the integrity value until the company had appraised business practices in 'dodgy' areas and put systems and protocols in place to prevent such circumstances ever arising again.*

---

# What criteria should a vision, mission or values meet?

Visions, missions and values should appeal to the heart as well as the head and should engender genuine commitment to align with the views stated. It must be remembered that well articulated visions and values help to focus people on the steps they need to take to **Do**, to **Have** or to **Become**. This is best summed up as a statement which has a precise and sharp clarity about specific desired outcomes.

To really benefit from such statements, it is important to satisfy these criteria:

- **Vision, mission and values are strongly customer-focused**

- **They should be challenging and inspiring**

- **Be easy to understand**

- **Straightforward and simple to articulate**

- **Go beyond one person's dream**

- **Evolve and not be frozen in time, unless circumstances demand a strong focus because of a 'life or death' issue facing the business.**

- **Provide a rationale or motivation for change and improvement**

On completion of vision, mission and values, the top team's objective is to win the support of all and. . .

**To commit to action to sharpen, intensify and deepen the vision, mission and values through communication.**

## Value building workshops

Part of our first day in any workshop is spent looking at the way major organisations have projected themselves in public. Marks & Spencer. Kwikfit, The Body Shop, Virgin, British Airways, Royal Mail (who have made significant progress for a public sector organisation), BP and many other companies are examined and their mission statements dissected. Many of those attending were surprised that these companies did not not say too much about their mission. Many did not have a mission statement but everyone knew what they stood for because they had projected what they believed into the market place and, most importantly, they lived their values. At this stage, the top team took ownership and agreed to work on a joint project which was to operate at two levels — the values clarification exercise.

**101**

## Values define behaviours

Initially we agree on core values to drive the business. These include customer focus, respect for the individual, integrity in business dealings, value for money, service, Quality and Excellence and teamwork. Then we focus on action verbs — what is it we want to do differently?

• In how many ways can these values be demonstrated?

• What specifically do we have to do more of?

• What do we have to continue doing?

• What do we have to stop doing?

• What current behaviours would deny our attempt to live the value?

If answers are forthcoming, they need to be shared with others in the organisation who will have the role of living and communicating the values to customers, staff at all levels and internal and external stakeholders or shareholders.

## Communication

In the public sector example introduced in this chapter to illustrate the points above, the top team decided they would commit to action. They ensured their direct reports went through the same two-day workshop and that the top team would explain how they progressed through the session. But first they committed to developing a draft document which became a powerful tool at the Values Clarification workshop which subsequently took place.

Direct reports contributed their views and a working group was established to polish up the documents and suggest the next steps. Before this happened other staff were selected — forming a diagonal slice of the business — to contribute their views and mission, values and behaviours were stated and agreed.

Through a complex communication process, everyone had a part to play in understanding what the values meant, what were the key drivers in shaping values and how values were translated into specific were to be encouraged. Training workshops were put in place to reflect values and behaviours that were to be displayed at a managerial and team player level.

## Summary and bullet points

Clarifying what a business stands for adds focus and direction. The purpose of identifying vision, mission and values enables emotion to be attached to direction. The values exercise is critical in shaping behaviours. Once people know what they need to do they can apply their natural energy and pattern to take action.

- Know the difference between vision, mission, values and behaviours.

- Consider the impact on the business which fails to give direction to its people

- How can people service the customer when, in their eyes, all they are doing is a job? Add some emotion to their role.

- Ensure your culture operates beyond the 'maintenance' level.

- Values give intellectual clarity and direction.

- What do you want to do, have and become?

- Align vision, mission and values with business strategy.

- Use data on the relative health of your business or organisation as an opportunity to improve rather than perceive it as unnecessary criticism.

- Use cultural reviews to test your business strategy for understanding.

- Treasure honesty in cultural reviews from staff. Identify all areas where improvement is desired.

- Constantly use the 9 S's framework for evaluating what you do as a business.

- Work from the top down to clarify values.

- Listen to views of others – the view from their perspective is of high value.

- Reject vague, casual statements in favour of real values which you commit to live.

- Espouse only that to which you will commit personally.

- Ensure that all statements are simple to understand, arouse passion and focus energy in one direction.

*Chapter 8 :*

# Walking the talk: leading Strategic Change

**'The degree to which your business will succeed or fail is dependent on what your leaders are, do and become.'**

When considering the strategies available for influencing and forming a strong culture, there is only one effective option which is to focus almost completely on the dominant style of management or leadership within the business. I much prefer the title 'leader' to 'manager' as it implies a much stronger position and role. 'Leader' implies ownership of concepts, taking charge, being action-oriented, influencing events, having a personal mission with responsibility as well as being a role model for others. The term 'manager', which can be restrictive in interpretation and imply a strong focus upon control, administration and co-ordination, generally appears to be more passive in nature and tends to avoid the proactive 'can do' element of true leaders. You will agree that organisations driven by leaders with strong positive values will take their organisations where others, driven by their passive counterpart, can only imagine.

It goes without saying that the quality of those who lead the business ultimately influences the quality of your achievements as a business. Just as a rugby or football coach gives careful consideration to the composition of his team, so the top team of any business should give attention to the composition, developments, core attributes and characteristics of the key players.

**105**

The key players will either be direct reports to the top team or part of the team who report to the most senior level within the organisation. So with an enterprise of 3,000 people, if you can positively influence the top 150 staff, you are in a strong position to improve business performance. This means that, just by focusing efforts on working with 0.5% of corporate staff, i.e. the top team and their direct reports, the natural outcome, if well designed, will influence activities of the whole business. A carefully-designed change strategy focused on the key players will significantly and radically improve corporate performance and success.

## To succeed you need quality leaders

The gains of this approach were illustrated while I was working with a major bank. This intervention as a simple case study will help guide us through the key issues. It will also focus upon the sequence of events in maximising potential for the business by working on changing the culture.

Initially, we worked with the top 50 of the 6,000 person, 380 branch organisation. Ten executives composed the top team, with the most senior staff comprising two tranches of managers who went through an intense and rigorous development process over 18 months. Because we were able to instil core concepts, primarily concerned with creating a 'customer-focused culture', we had enormous leverage on bank activities. In the culture change initiative (CCI), a series of long-term team projects focused on changing culture within the bank. All delivered success.

## A case study : The bank strategy for culture change

The top team was driven by a powerful and charismatic managing director and over several days we discussed the causal factors which we believed impacted upon positive change. The top team committed to undertake a rigorous, speedy review of the culture.

After conducting a survey through one-to-one interviews with key people, by running focus groups and interviewing key players at head office and throughout the branch network, we created a 'gap analysis'. This provided a detailed outline of how we were going to move from 'where we are today' to 'the Bank we want to become'.

## Role Models: Banc One

The bank had a role model which it wished to emulate in terms of performance. This was determined by what it was possible to achieve in the financial services industry. The selected role model was Banc One, in the United States, which had turned around its business and developed a strategic approach towards winning customers. One measure was related to cross-selling of services within the bank. Each customer held or consumed 3.1 Banc One services. In comparison, in Europe, the average customer of the average bank consumed or purchased only 1.3 bank products or services. Clearly there was a significant difference between current performance and what was possible. There were many other benefits which could accrue to my client, if they, like Banc One, could master the culture which would promote cross selling throughout their customer base. Cross Selling in retrospect was one issue where there were many.

The top team undertaking the change understood that they offered just as many services and products as any of their competitors. But they were failing to sell those services to prospective customers and existing clients.

To illustrate the point further, I had been a customer of the bank, my client, for more than 15 years and had a corporate account for over ten years. But not once had a sales executive approached me to offer other bank services such as a lease for computers, a business telephone system, motor vehicles, short-term business loans, a pension. I had received plenty of junk mail advertising these services but not once had my bank manager picked up the phone and taken the initiative to win more business. Yet I was a consumer of all these products, over many years – with other providers. I can honestly say that it really does not matter to me where I purchase these services. And I am also sure if I had been asked to consider the purchase from the bank my answer probably would have been yes. But the enquiries never came, the phone calls were never made and the bank manager and his staff did not fulfil their potential to cross-sell extra services. How many other account holders could have also been cross-sold extra services?

The organisation's biggest challenge was to move staff from just managing the business towards leading and growing it. The major barrier was to be some of the key players in the process of delivering customer service – the managers of the bank. They did not see themselves as salesmen. They preferred their less-than-active role as advisors on personal or financial matters; or lenders who appraised the credit worthiness of proposals. Their role was perceived as passive and analytic, rather than proactive and commercially focused.

## Leaders not managers

The bank could have been far more successful even if they sold existing services, with vigour, to customers. This cross-selling would be very powerful if it led to increased profitability for the bank and helped increase customer loyalty. For instance, if the average consumption of bank services was less than two products per customer, there was enormous scope for improvement.

To all intent and purposes, business success was dependent on the perception which each manager had of the role he should play in the business. If he saw himself as an administrator, solely attending to risk assessment and accountability, that is what he would become. If however, he saw himself as a commercial extension of the business, with personal profit and loss accountability, he would be more outgoing and go-getting

In reality, the success of the bank's customer service strategy, which existed by default at that time, fell squarely upon the perceived role of each of the 380 managers who ran their business units or branches. There was one major problem. Although some were clearly focused and lived up to the commercial expectations and realities of life, not all managers wanted to, or felt a commitment to, become sales-oriented. As several managers said disdainfully "I did not join the bank (in the 1960s) to become a salesman".

So the problem was easily stated: how to introduce a strong customer-focused strategy into the business when the vast majority of staff in key influential positions do not have the commitment, confidence, skills or desire to fulfil the requirements of the role or grow into the role?

## Role models : a mindset shift

Overall, the really successful bank manager should not manage detailed elements of the bank – that could be completed with others with supervisory and administrative skills. The real driver would be the person with a strong commercial and business drive. He or she would visit customers, not reside all the time in their bank.

At the time some, pioneers of change argued that a good driver should spend one day a week co-ordinating events in the bank and four days out selling. What a shake up in roles.

## A strategy for change

Without going into details, the real drivers behind any change had to come from the top. I therefore started to build an active programme which would maximise the potential of those reporting to the top team.

First, we committed to an action learning programme. I am particularly critical of change programmes based on passive learning; in this programme there was a strong emphasis on working together. We committed to this approach:

To provide four workshops to examine key issues in organisational change. Each workshop would be led by experts and key contributors, practitioners of change. Practitioners means in this context people who had implemented and owned the change process and who would introduce each subject and discuss relevant research and its implications for rapid implementation. The only consultant was myself. Issues would be debated and leading practitioners would contribute views.

In every workshop we ensured that every manager would visit an organisation which had succeeded in specific change areas. The purpose of these visits was to expose managers to other cultures and other organisations, thus giving them a good understanding of the dynamics of change. I visited and exchanged views with many companies, including GE Plastics, a dynamic aspect of General Electric in the United States, and the Royal Mail. The bank and Royal Mail found they had something in common: large groups of staff on whom the senior teams depended to deliver to their customer base. Both organisations had staff and customers; each could learn best practices from the other.

## Mindset shifts and thinking outside the box

Those who attended the programme were encouraged to arrange their own visits to other largely successful businesses, resulting in learning a great deal about customer service from companies such as Marks & Spencer and BP, as well as legal and insurance businesses. More importantly, managers started to explore how other companies developed and implemented change management strategies. By going outside their field of experience, they expand their horizons and understanding.

We wanted to create a shift in mindset to see how things could be 'outside the box'. We wanted managers to become, as Tom Peters suggests, 'creative swipers', swiping and innovating ideas from other businesses and implementing them with their own. We wanted them to move out of their comfort zones and stretch their skills. This was achieved through setting up project teams.

## Strategic cross-functional teams

IT managers worked with sales staff, credit managers and senior banking staff. They were tasked to choose a project to which they would commit to deliver over a nine to 12 months, allocating two days a month to the project. Their seniority would require them to agree, delegate or negotiate with others to do those things they would no longer have time for. The project must be of their choosing and have significant impact on the bank in terms of delivering and sustaining a customer-focused culture and impacting positively on commercial performance. The objective was not to be a 'nice culture' but to impact directly upon the business.

Each team's sponsor would open gates and provide inspiration and resource. The sponsor was a senior member of the top team and would only sponsor projects which were not his direct responsibility. This was to ensure that sponsors would not intervene with their 'pet' solution to the project. Team projects included delivering a sales and service strategy; living the values; benchmarking 'best in class'; reduction in rework or failure costs; process re-engineering; communication and many others. Apart from team facilitation, as and when required, the groups would be self-managing. They would regularly report progress to the CEO and his top team.

Output from workshops and groups was immense – and extremely positive. It cannot be over-emphasised how much impact these groups had on others. For instance, the Process re-engineering group trained more than 100 staff in problem solving and process mapping in order that they could help facilitate local problem-solving groups throughout the branch network. This was of great benefit to the changing culture. After training, the potential of the 100 additional people expanded rapidly; their thoughts, words and actions were listened to and implemented. Literally dozens of events were soon emerging. Working with less than 1% of the 6000 workforce, the bank began to see results right through the organisation. The domino effect was apparent – learnings from one group were transferred to others. The ideas and actions behind culture change was taking hold.

# High impact, low profile strategy

So what was the strategy and why was it successful? Unlike too many change initiatives, it was not given a noisy and powerful launch, with endless publicity and meaningless slogans. It was a low profile, action oriented initiative which would impact on the business and provide a powerful foundation upon which other more specialised projects would rise and flourish. Most importantly there would be a common language and understanding between those who had taken part in the programme. They had been exposed to new and vibrant ideas and experiences. They had not just heard about new approaches to change and relevant research. They had heard from practitioners of change. They had witnessed how change had been implemented in other companies. And they had committed two days a month to a strategic project.

# Summary and bullet points

When implementing change on a practical level, you need to start at the top and use key players as change agents. But this cannot be done unless you provide the right environment. You have to commit to whatever it takes to remove individuals from their comfort zones and expand their horizons. You have to expose them to best practices and to new cultures. Not by reading about them, but by visiting, by questioning, by working with other change agents and committing to joint projects. This the rest is easy – you just have to agree on what skills and competencies, attitudes and mindsets will help you achieve this performance, then inculcate them in your staff.

- Leaders have vision and direction. Managers control and administer. Which will cause change to take place most successfully in your business?

- Managers live in the here and now, leaders are future-oriented, independent, have strong opinions and make things happen. Knowing how commercial work is changing, who do you want to manage the vast majority of your business and provide demanding customers with the service they require?

- Nowadays, companies need transformational staff who are committed to change.

- Companies still need transactional people to manage interfaces and attend to detail. But these people should never be given strategic responsibility to the detriment of transformers.

- Leaders are developed through training and being stretched beyond their current performance. There is danger in staying within the 'comfort zone'.

- Others have implemented change initiatives which will work within your business. Expose yourselves to best practices.

- Look at what works for others and adapt it for your circumstances.

- Set up cross-functional teams to examine organisation problems and roadblocks. All cultural problems need to be understood from a variety of perspectives.

- Commit to developing your top five per cent of people to become masters of change.

*Chapter 9:*

# Shaping the Strategic Leader

## So what makes a good leader?

If you read my book, *Creating Culture Change*, chapter six outlines many of the theories about, and approaches to leadership behaviour. We do not have time to go through the 350 definitions of leadership, but I will go through the key issues which I believe makes a good leader. In training workshops we spend countless hours developing skills by working through case material and conducting role plays geared to improve inter-personal competence. This supports my strong belief that leaders are made, not born. What follows highlights the action that can be taken to develop quality leadership, for without leadership there is no change.

Given motivation, anyone can improve their performance but they need a strong and positive attitude to get the most out of training.

Leadership is a science and an art which can be continually improved. With the right temperament to learning, with a commitment to practise skills, any person can become a great leader and achieve anything he or she wishes. But change starts with examining personal values.

## Values and leadership behaviour

A leader needs an ability to look honestly at his own values and how they impact on his behaviour. How can you learn to lead others if you do not understand that values drive motivations and your own behaviour?

The degree of positive self-discovery is important in helping leaders shape their behaviours and think through core values. It's not enough to know your core values and understand how they impact on your behaviour. What is important is to understand that you can change your values; as these change, so does your behaviour. Values can change and evolve through circumstances in which we find ourselves, through our positive self-renewal.

Let us see how circumstances change personal values. Take, for instance, the values of a single male aged mid to late twenties who has been through University and started in business. At this age, his values may be strongly focused on his career so they may be achievement-oriented and careerist in nature. Now take that same individual, provide him with a partner, two children and add four years to his life. He will have different values because the critical incidents and 'circumstances' which have impacted upon him will have changed his view of the world. In other words, his relative priorities will have changed. The responsibility of a partner or wife, two children demands on his work time, his family and studies will have shaped and changed him. How he behaves now may well be very different from the man at a younger age.

It is important to understand how critical incidents in your life impact upon you. You may never understand the dynamics and all the causal factors which shape the way things turn out. But at least if you understand what is happening, you can take preventative action to manage transitions, ie for yourself and for others. The values which you hold will shape your behaviour and you can probably trace how your values have changed over time.

Values can also change by design rather than through circumstances. Perhaps certain values will hold people back from achieving their potential or there is a conflict of values. For instance some people have conflict between wanting to be liked and generally demonstrating affection with others with whom they work at the same time as rising up the managerial ladder. To some there may tend to be a conflict. 'How can I be a manager telling people what to do and also be well liked?' There isn't a conflict; it's just a perception that one excludes the other. This person will have to come to terms with the element of the managerial role which denotes 'control or regulation' and will have to develop some rules – like always being fair and equitable when dealing with others. This review or reframe of a situation effect, changes the person's values and behaviour. Because he is looking at the same issue from a different angle, his depth of understanding of what is important will also change.

Perhaps when a person takes up his their first managerial or leadership role, there is a shock when they have to deal with an issue of poor performance. The experience, which may be less than positive, will impact upon their view of the world. The person, realising they do not possess all the skills of an effective leader or coach, may purposely seek these skills. To be successful in seeking to develop and apply skills, you must value them. People do what they value – and value what they do. We are all continually seeking to improve the way we do things; the different perceptions we develop shape our values, hopefully for the better. So what values should be portrayed by a manager or leader of people? It is not easy to list them but obviously it would be advantageous to actually value the contribution of others and enjoy working with people. It is important to think through the values that are important to you in getting the job done.

## Eliciting leadership values

- **Think of a person whom you admire and who you believe leads effectively. Write down the values that you understand, that drive the person's behaviour. Now rank order these values.**

- **Write down your own values and rank order them. Now compare your values to those of your 'role model' above. Identify consistencies and areas for your personal development.**

- **Now agree what experiences and events you must pursue in order to develop these values. Once you have focused upon these, work on them.**

Our values as human beings or leaders are shaped by experiences. By shaping these experiences, and involving ourselves in new ways of working, our wisdom in leading others grows.

An example demonstrates how effective this can be. A female training manager in her thirties had the potential to become the human resources director for her company. However, she was perceived as being too inexperienced in the broader issues of HR. I asked the managing director what experience – not training – she would need to perform well in the new role. He stated these clearly, relating them to the changes which were going to affect the company. From this discussion, we devised a series of placements with other businesses, who would host the young woman to work on fairly high-powered projects, delivering to the top team. She probably learned more in a four-month period working with three other businesses than throughout her own career. By exposing her to new organisations, different contexts and new business cultures, she learned quickly. She was speedily promoted to the post of HR Director and demonstrated her wisdom almost immediately.

**'People are shaped not by what happens to them but how they respond to what happened to them.'**

Developing learning around situations and experiences does more to mould leadership and managerial values than training alone. Training is all very well in shaping behaviour but exposure to dealing with change is longer lasting and more effective.

## Those who influence and lead

There are three types of people: those who are active and influence and shape events; those who are passive and are influenced; and those who say 'what happened?' True leaders need to be of the first category in order to succeed and achieve. They need to know how they work in order to help others work more effectively.

This level of critical analysis needs to be positive in outlook. A phrase which I love, and believe we should all gravitate towards, is to become a 'tough-minded optimist'. Tough-minded because we need to look realistically at events and people – without being drawn into the inner world of 'self doubt', but also, optimist, because, generally speaking, things do tend to work out okay. We can thus be optimistic because we know we have control over how we influence others and can always make good things happen. Influence is an important key to leadership.

## Self critical – what's it like to receive my behaviour?

Managers who lack social skills are on a losing streak. Those who have not captured the essence of inter-personal influence, rapport building, coaching and discussion leading will not be able to facilitate themselves out of a paper bag. Gone are the days of rigid control and regulation. We work in a world in which there is greater mobility between roles in companies. Leaders and managers are under intense pressure not just to attract good people to their company but to retain them – and their loyalty.

**Research conducted six years ago suggested the second major factor why people moved to other jobs was that they did not like working for their boss.**

The first factor was positive and related to wanting to progress and achieve in their career. But the second factor is of concern to companies having difficulty holding on to their best talent. Creating a positive climate is central. Leaders should look in the mirror from time to time and ask 'how I am doing?'

When starting a session on leadership I sometimes give everybody a small mirror and ask them to look into it. While they are looking at their own reflection I ask them to be honest with themselves and say out loud....

- **What's it like to work for me?**

- **What does it feel like receiving my critical comments – especially when I'm in a bad mood?**

- **How can I be a more effective leader?**

These questions are critical when assessing personal development needs. So we are asking for a more self-critical approach.

If you can 'read' yourself, you are more likely to 'read' others. A strong behavioural approach manifests itself in understanding the dynamics and motivation of why people act as they do, and asking questions:

- **Why did that happen?**

- **What did they do?**

- **What has to happen so that I can achieve X?**

- **In how many ways can I win the support of my team to Y?**

By being curious about their relationships with others, managers can learn more about themselves. And we learn more about ourselves when we learn how we react and work with others.

## 360 degree assessments

In some organisations, managers commit to 360 degree assessments which are powerful in generating data on working with others. If these are conducted in an honest and confidential manner, they work really well — but this is not always the case. Seeking feedback from staff, colleagues and the boss is helpful — but what is done with the information is much more important. We regularly conduct this process with management teams and find it an incredibly powerful process in changing behaviour when working with teams.

## Behavioural and intellectual curiosity

I am always gratified when managers show a genuine interest in applying theory. I don't think enough managers are aware of the tremendous degree of contemporary research conducted in organisational behaviour; too many are exposed to too little. Managers need to understand that the 'art and science' of leadership requires an enquiring mind to know, and to want to learn, about how others manage their business. This will only happen if managers go out of their way to read, attend seminars, and commit to understand that they can manage more effectively. They can do this not by trial and error but by study and by setting themselves their own personal development plan.

## Leadership = energy + focus

Leadership is about two factors which can be broken down further, but it is basically to do with harnessing personal energy and focusing it in a positive direction. People who possess boundless energy are driven by passions which get them up early and keep them up till late. People who have energy create energy with those with whom they come into contact . They can inspire others to boost their energy.

Leaders who lack energy are slow. Their body language is boring, uninteresting and uninspirational. Managers with negative energy need to be kept well away from customers because they do not inspire confidence. If you owned the business, you would ensure that anyone in a leadership position possessed massive energy. For with energy comes enthusiasm.

Energy is powerful. But aligned with a focused direction it is extremely powerful. Know where you are going and you'll probably get there before anyone else. If you are not sure where you are going you will probably get lost on the way, and stumble from one business failure to another. Few people plan their lives and even fewer plan their careers. Those that do reap the rewards.

## Research into leadership

Research tells us that effective managers spend most of their time in five specific activities. Kouzes and Posner's research suggests that managers who visibly **challenge the way things are done**, and who continually look for new ways to solve old problems, tend to be prized as leaders. They are impatient for change: always looking, continually striving to do things better, faster and cheaper.

These same managers will go to any lengths to **inspire themselves, and others**, to achieve unbelievable targets.

They will **enable people to act**, providing their teams and individuals with opportunities to develop skills and expertise.

They will **model the behaviour** they want others to adopt and lead from the front.

Finally, managers perceived as true leaders use **praise and recognition to support the team**.

Praise is a powerful behaviour but not always part of the average manager's kit bag of skills. We often spend time talking through praise and what can be done to improve 'praising skills.' Many of us spend our time looking for what is wrong in a situation rather than what is right. This critical, negative approach is of little value. We need to become more positive and praising what people have done beyond normal expectations and standards.

Praise has to be genuine. If it is not genuine, and not delivered with congruence, it's a waste of time. People know when a manager is being genuine and when he is just going through the motions. People look for congruence with what you say, your body language, tone of your words and how you act immediately before and after delivery of the praise. They know intuitively whether the praise is sincere or not.

To be effective, praise for the person who did the outstanding work must be given as close to the event as possible. Waiting six months for a company conference to praise the efforts of several people will not have the impact it could have. Delivering the good news and recognising performance in the same week will reinforce the individual's behaviour and be more effective.

Praise has to be delivered with feeling, but many managers have difficulty discussing their feelings. They need to be able to articulate how they are affected by a person behaving beyond that prescribed. It may give you confidence in the person, knowing that you can always trust their ability. Their behaviour could make you feel proud and lucky to work with a person of such calibre; or it may instil in you the want to learn some of the skills displayed by the person recognised.

What is important is that these behaviours, especially praise, have to be learned. This requires the leader to look at his role and understand that he, too, has a steep learning curve to follow.

## Learn to love change

Leaders need to love change and consider transition management a core responsibility. Anyone in a leadership position should be skilled and versed in change management techniques and be able to operate on the boundaries between different cultures. It also requires a personal commitment to consider that he is to give direction and focus to ambiguous circumstances. He has to become a master of change.

## Planning and prevention

It is helpful to be able to manage time. There is never enough time to do everything but the manager who has focus will make time for important priorities. The leader will spend a great deal of his time preventing problems arising, rather than fixing things after they have gone wrong. How can we create a powerful culture if we fail to master time?

## Team-driven

Leaders are strongly team-driven and should have the capacity to work across boundaries. Working with a team focus requires a commitment to the desired outcome, which is customer-focused. To support the customer focus, we need a strong commitment to maximising the processes and infrastructure which delivers to customers. Moving and dealing with 'turf wars' and managing team dynamics is critical to success.

## Integrity

Personal integrity is essential. Ethical conduct, fairness and firmness when necessary, are the hallmark of a leader who is respected by others. The leader can only win respect by enabling the team to achieve their needs.

## Summary and bullet points

Leadership is the issue which will determine whether you succeed in mastering the potential of your business. A company devoid of leaders is unlikely to survive and certainly will not maximise and lever the power of its employees. Empowerment rests on leaders nurturing people to achieve unbelievable performance standards.

- Anyone can learn anything if they have the motivation.

- Leaders are shaped and developed through experience and training – no-one is born a leader.

- Personal values guide leadership behaviour.

- Self-discovery lies at the foundation of developing leadership potential.

- Values change. Circumstances, and how you respond to them, shape leadership values.

- Values beget behaviour.

- You can change your values through exposing yourself to learning experiences.

- Values can change quickly, depending on the criticality of the change.

- Learn to elicit your own values and compare them to the values of those you consider leadership role models.

- There are those who influence and lead; those who stand by, watch, then respond; and those who say 'what happened?'. Which leaders do you have in your business?

- Ask these questions: What is it like to receive my behaviour? What is it like to work with me if I am in a bad mood?

- To examine your behaviour, commit to a 360 degree assessment, then commit to act on the results.

- What should you do more of to enable others…. and what should you do less to stop inhibiting others?

- Curiosity is one of the most powerful desires associated with developing yourself and others.

- Be intellectually curious. Start reading into organisational behaviour.

- Leadership = energy + focus.

- Energy and enthusiasm is infectious. They stimulate others to perform well.

- Be a self-confident, tough-minded optimist.

- Add focus to energy and align your values and behaviour.

- Challenge the ways things are done.

- Inspire others.

- Commit to over-train your staff. You won't succeed.

- Lead by example.

- Find someone doing something right, then tell them.

- Deliver genuine praise with vigour. Use your feeling to recognise great performance among your staff.

- Change is your greatest ally – it enables leaders to use their skills.

- Focus upon prevention and work as a team leader and facilitator.

- Lead with integrity.

- Without leadership there is no change.

# Chapter 10:

# The motivational calculus

**In the average organisation, the word empowerment is overused, misunderstood and practised infrequently.**

Before we can promote empowerment as a concept, we need to understand the underpinning and foundation upon which it will flourish. There are several key issues which need to be addressed. Fundamentally, empowerment as a concept will not evolve until managers learn how to motivate staff. The magic buttons which need to be pressed, which will enliven staff, and create that zap of 'personal responsibility,' can only be accessed when key business leaders understand the complexity of the motivational equation. Understanding what motivates is insufficient. A high degree of unconscious competence is also required. Then the manager or leader can automatically apply, with ease, techniques and tools for channelling the potential of his people. If managers fail to practise these motivational skills and new approaches, the good ideas will never become part of that person's repertoire of behaviours.

Likewise, applying the same new technique with all direct reports will gain a manager the reputation of being stereotyped in his approach. Blandly applying one motivational technique to everyone in the business will undoubtedly fail. Over-application of any one fad will soon be recognised by staff as an inflexible style of management. And staff are aware that when managers have attended the latest training event they tend to blindly overuse what they have learned. You will be aware of the case where a new management fad has been over-sold - because on their return from the workshop managers will over-apply the same techniques time and time again. To combat this concern, and to motivate staff effectively, managers at all levels need to

**125**

understand the psychology of individual differences. This is why we spent time discussing the rationality and approach to leadership in the last two chapters.

---

*You can't have TQ until you have quality of management*

*Some time ago a large manufacturing business requested that we conduct a feasibility study for a Total Quality initiative. We found that the majority of senior managers and supervisors had not attended any form of development training for ten years. Events or programmes had been geared almost exclusively to technical applications of technology.*

*It appeared that, over the ten-year period, the top team had not paid any attention to developments in organisational behaviour and change to enable them appraise how they ran their business. However they had become excited about Total Quality - wrongly confusing it with a major cost reduction exercise.*

*In this company, management was strictly a control function and morale and motivation was at an all time low. After five days meeting with, and debating, the role of change, we concluded the company should not commit to Quality until managers understood the role they should play in developing their staff. Any investment in Quality improvement would be wasted because managers did not know how best to motivate their people. When we produced a report of progress highlighting a requirement for radical improvement, we clearly stated that, under no circumstances, should this business commit to a TQ initiative until the quality of managers was improved. We concluded that the top two layers of management be assessed as a team and substantial investment be undertaken to bring understanding and application of sound leadership and managerial behaviour up to speed.*

*Issue*

*How many businesses suffer from similar problems?*

---

# Ideas on motivation

Before we can have empowerment, leaders need to know how to lead and motivate. Much has been written on motivation but little has been applied. Clearly it is important to look at the motivational equation. The manager or leader must have the capability to motivate and lead, which means he understands the approaches to be taken. This requires the leader to choose from a variety of approaches and blend his application with a variety of styles. Individual differences require the leader/manager to adopt a contingent style; this will be influenced by a variety of factors.

# Contingent motivational style

Before motivating anyone, it is important to look at the 'target person' and understand his/her 'personal psychology.' Adopting a flexible approach and tailoring motivation to the person is critical to success. One to one coaching, listening and praising may be a variant that would work with one staff member; others require focus and direction, rather than time and debate. It really depends on the person. Perhaps the role of manager is moving towards that of a facilitator, using a myriad of influencing styles and strategies to get the most out of people.

The leader must take two issues into account:

### What motivates?

### How to motivate?

Absence of either of these two complementary core issues in motivation will produce a one-sided result in any organisation. Knowing and understanding the variety of factors to motivate people is critical but it is also important to understand the motivational process. We need to understand that the personal values of the individual will be a major factor in the equation. By establishing and discussing personal values, it is possible to find out what is important to that person. People who place a high value on involvement will be driven to higher degrees of performance by a leader who gives them the responsibility to become a major player in key projects. It is up to the leader to decide what constitutes being a major player. Does it encompass responsibility in decision-making, a core role in implementation? The first step is understanding the values that drive the person.

# Understand a person's values, then motivate accordingly.

Everyone is driven by different things. As we evolve, our needs will change. This is governed by our values. We do what we value and we value what we do. By eliciting a person's values, we may understand how people tick. As a person evolves, and as his or her circumstances change, the values change. So what is important to a single 25-year-old technician will not necessarily reflect what is important to him when he is 32, a husband and father of two young children.

This highlights the complexity of human behaviour and argues the case that anyone who manages people needs to understand human nature. To really get to grips with the man management issue, a manager or leader needs to spend more time listening. Only by listening to what others say, and what they have difficulty saying, does a man manager really learn how to motivate.

As part of the performance assessment process, or day-to-day management and discussion, it is important that every manager learns to ask the following questions and listen carefully to the response.

- **What is important to you in doing your job or performing your role?**

- **What do I need to do to enable you to perform more effectively?**

- **What conditions do I need to create to enable you to feel a high degree of job satisfaction?**

Motivation is dependent on two people: the person motivating and the needs of the person to be motivated. So what conditions do we need to understand to do an even better job at motivating staff to achieve potential?

## Motivation: towards and away from

Some people are motivated by being drawn towards a desired goal; others are motivated by becoming distant from an undesirable state. For instance, some are motivated to work hard and contribute because they want to be admired and respected - they crave recognition. So the goal of recognition is enough to spur them on. If they can see an opportunity where their contribution is valued, and they value praise and recognition, that can be sufficient motivation. However, there are people who seek recognition but in a reverse form. They fear criticism so they will do the best they can to avoid, or move away from, negative comments from their boss. They will create a situation where negative comments are totally avoided. Put another way, some people are driven by avoiding pain, others by seeking pleasure. The 'avoidance of pain' person will contribute a great deal to his or her work because of the awful things could happen if he does not. For instance the pain principle works on 'what will happen to you if you don't do X' It's not my favourite motivational tactic but many people are, by nature, 'away from' and 'avoiding pain' in their motivation. An acquaintance used to motivate himself in his business by buying a new car, having an expensive holiday and committing to purchases which he could ill afford. This, he would tell me, would act as a motivator to achieve unbelievable performance levels with his customers and attract new business. This negative view of motivation is clearly not desired and is very stressful. Some people are driven in this way, whereas others are driven by the thought of a positive, compelling future.

---

*Pain or Pleasure?*

*Ask yourself...*

*What situations or circumstances do you avoid at all costs? This is your 'away from' motivation.*

*What situations or circumstances do you seek for personal gratification? This is your 'towards' motivation.*

*Work through each of your direct reports and colleagues thinking through their 'towards' and 'away' situations. You will learn a great deal about how to motivate them.*

---

In reality most people are a mixture of 'pain' and 'pleasure'. A person who is too much driven by 'pain' will find motivation a little stressful; the 'pleasure' only people may find they spend too much time focusing on dreams which are not always realistic. Try to understand why people do the things they do.

## What motivates?

Let's deal with the key factors. As we understand the cultural iceberg and its different layers, we note that people have their own motivational iceberg. Needs require to be satisfied before moving on to more sophisticated motivations. It is well acknowledged that we generally move from simple to quite complex motivations. The gratification of our needs does not follow a preordained sequence, as Abraham Maslow suggested, in a hierarchy moving from simple to complex needs. But it is a tidy explanation of how some people are motivated.

*Diagram 6. Diagram Maslow*

# Diagram Maslow

The most basic needs of all, physiological in nature, include food, drink and sex. Researchers would suggest that, once these have been satiated, the human being moves up the hierarchy to higher order needs. These needs are met in the workplace through rewards associated with working, namely pay or money. Once these needs have been met, the individual is said to operate on a higher plane, then gravitate towards 'shelter needs' – that is protection from the environment – ensuring protection against unfavourable conditions. In most situations this includes financial protection, could be translated as a pension, financial security or insurance. Clearly, these needs can also be met through the pay cheque.

Money and terms and conditions of employment, which satisfy the most basic needs of the individual, are often the only motivator used by organisations. Human beings are driven by a variety of needs and motivations. These higher order needs, often misunderstood by organisations, are often never used.

Man has a need to be part of a larger grouping or team. Some people are driven strongly by association while others are more selective, while still seeking some association. Hence we have extroverts who love the company of others; and introverts, who are more selective. 'Social contact' is important for most people. Depriving people of such contact with others can be demotivating and stressful. Please note the failure of many 'working from home' initiatives which have collapsed because there is a need for people to affiliate.

Becoming part of a working team, developing a team identity and performing roles within that team will motivate people far beyond the strict specialisation of labour roles. These roles are often dictated by mass production businesses in which technology solely determines the degree of social interaction.

Moving from simple to complex we find that recognition, responsibility, being self directed and valued for contributions become a major motivator for most people. The pinnacle of motivation is to be 'self actualising', creative, self directing and master of your own destiny achieving full potential. This is what all people aspire to but the level of satisfaction in working lives is open to debate.

It is obvious that if a manager or leader understands the process, the 'what motivates' components, he will be more likely to make the transition and ensure that the needs of staff are integrated with organisational objectives. In that way harmony is achieved.

However, it is important to understand what conditions allow people to enjoy a high degree of satisfaction in their job. It will come as no surprise that those factors which motivate tend to be concerned with meeting 'higher order' needs. The factors that maintain people in their roles tend to answer 'lower order' needs. For instance, staff may not have a high degree of job satisfaction because there is little opportunity to display and meet their recognition or self esteem needs. But they stay at work because pay and conditions are sufficient to maintain some degree of commitment and motivation. The absence of these factors would create circumstances in which these people would move on to other roles in other businesses.

Increasing pay and introducing new terms and conditions favourable to staff will not enhance job satisfaction but will reduce dis-satisfaction with the job. Hertzerg was the first amongst many to highlight that job satisfaction and dis-satisfaction are not opposites. What causes a decrease in dis-satisfaction does not necessarily motivate. More money does not mean more motivation. More money gives people more reasons to maintain their job but it does not necessarily induce a heightened emotional state or improvement to performance.

Companies that work on designing to increase intrinsic elements of a job, rather than working on extrinsic elements, will achieve a great deal more when working on maximising potential. It is important to work on 'higher order' needs and focus designing more responsibility into the job.

What does this tell us about creating an empowering culture? That people are extremely complex, driven by psychological as well as economic needs. It tells us that we must understand the dynamics of the individual if you are to exploit potential to do things better. It also suggests that, if we develop this view of staff with all our managers and business leaders, they will be in a stronger position to master potential.

## Motivation: the process

We can understand what motivates people to reach extraordinary performance but we must get the process right. Guiding principles are located in stimulus-response relationships. It is important that people understand and see the link between events and rewards. You may have worked in a business where reward was a function of long service. If people have little control to influence events so that they can become part of the motivational calculus, then they will only contribute what is required to maintain their employment. They will not be spurred on to achieve beyond mediocre performance standards.

People need to equate inputs with what they get out of the job. If there is little link between inputs and outputs, the drive to excel will not exist. It is imperative that these conditions are met.

The person is equipped with the skills and abilities to perform the role. There should be the opportunity to improve skills which lead to improved performance.

Job performance is possible and realistic, the normal outcome from performing core activities.

Rewards on offer are attractive and valued by those performing the job. Develop a reward, remuneration and recognition strategy which is desired by all.

There is a direct link between performing a job to the agreed standard, and beyond, and receiving the desired rewards. If there is a strong and direct causal link between 'performance' and 'reward', motivation will be high.

If all these conditions are met, there is every likelihood that motivation can be aroused. This approach has been termed the 'expectancy' theory, suggesting a strong causal link which will drive specific behaviours.

However, many organisations do not organise themselves on these lines. They fail to provide staff with the skills and training to perform to given standards. The link between performance and reward is tentative at most and the rewards on offer only partially attractive to staff.

Organisations which commit to developing rounded reward strategies that go beyond typical salary review and pension packages, and focus upon recognition and advancement, will reap the rewards. Simple ideas on content and process can, if applied, generate a motivated and empowered workforce.

## Summary and bullet points

Successful businesses will need a deep understanding of influence and motivation and just how it can be applied. Leaders who are equipped to read, understand and work through and apply motivational issues will be in a stronger position to create a culture in which empowerment is the norm. Tailoring solutions to staff is critical and forces managers to spend more time coaching, leading and team building than doing the job.

- Motivation in many companies is more by accident than design.

- Managers are paid to manage their people to achieve results and need a thorough understanding of core motivational principles and theories.

- What motivates will depend upon who we are trying to motivate, their circumstances, their situation and their individual psychology.

- First elicit a person's values, then understand their motivations.

- People are motivated to 'avoid' some circumstances and are 'attracted' to others. Use 'toward' and 'away from' motivation.

- Understand that we all have our personal hierarchy of motivations.

- What reduces dis-satisfaction with a job is not the same as what satisfies.

- Work on meeting the higher order needs of people to motivate them.

- Design for satisfying jobs by working on the 'intrinsic' nature of the job, rather than 'extrinsic' or 'external' factors.

- Ensure that reward is attractive and development a comprehensive recognition strategy linked to advancement.

- If performance in the job does not lead to reward, redesign your rewards strategy.

- Think of developing the whole person to integrate their needs with your objectives.

*Chapter 11:*

# Empowerment – in pursuit of the Holy Grail

The concept of empowerment is much misunderstood. There is a great deal of confusion about the term. True empowerment was alluded to earlier when we proposed that "if you couldn't fail, what would you like your organisation to look like and how would people operate?" Some managers believe empowerment is no more than flexible delegation. It is not. Delegation implies that control resides with the manager. An empowered culture is one where people know the boundaries of their work and who demonstrate their competence and confidence to take charge and responsibility to achieve the goals of the business. Empowerment is an end state where people take responsibility for their part of the business and are committed to working with others to help achieve them their goals. Here are some of the major components of empowerment.

## Broad Boundaries

An empowered individual will not have rigid limits on his specific job responsibilities. He will have flexibility in how he determines his role and his function. There is a degree of flexibility in defining the boundaries within which he works. Rigid job descriptions are archaic, restrictive and rejected. Because they tell people what they do and what they should not do, it is better to have key result areas. These areas are incredibly helpful in getting people to think more strategically and take them away from obsession with detail. Key result areas also focus on outcomes. What is the desired outcome of your work and how will it impact on overall performance?

**135**

## Expenditure of time and energy

It is better for the business to negotiate key result areas with its people than to prescribe job performance precisely. People should be given an indication of where their energy is to be expended and on what key results. So, for instance, the time allocation for four projects may be for 1) 40%; for 2) 30%; for 3) 20%; and 4) 10%. The allocation indicates the relative importance of these projects. Certainly, the employee will realise that, on average, he needs to devote probably two days per week to the first project and only hours to the low priority project. Empowerment is dependent upon developing staff and managers equally. It cannot exist just at one level – it is a process and an end in itself. Empowered staff flourish when managers stop controlling and start facilitating progress.

## Changing the perceived role and self esteem of the job

Some organisations have made what may appear to be trivial attempts to empower through changing job titles. For example from 'order clerk' to 'sales consultant' may appear to be changing only the surface structure of the role. But I have seen marked changes in the role and self-presentation of people performing in the newly-styled job. This I witnessed at a brewery where staff would phone public houses and ask for their order for the following weeks. Changing the job title changed the perceived role of the people who performed this task. They thought of themselves in a stronger position, far more active than passive. Three of a team of 12 asked to attend a telephone sales training course to enable them to more effectively compete for the monthly incentives which, in the past, had not been deemed attractive to them.

I have also seen this strategy work wonders with a senior sales manager whose title became vice president of European and North American Sales. His performance went though the roof and his self esteem rocketed. When he presented his card, made a phone call, sent an email or letter, customers knew they were communicating with a senior person in a powerful position. Do not underestimate the power of changing the perceived role. We all make assumptions about the scope of a person's job, the authority and relative power to influence decisions. Changing from passive descriptions of jobs, like 'wages clerks' to 'incentives team' can have a profound effect on a person's self esteem. There are those who scorn the idea but any action which heightens the scope of any role should be considered as a step to empowerment.

Some companies have given individuals and teams the opportunity to rename their positions, their job titles and their functions, with the surprising effect that performance increases. Other companies refuse to give people job titles because they believe it immediately restricts the scope of people and the role they play. Self esteem is an important driving factor for most people. Any attempt to genuinely impact upon, and improve self esteem, has got to be of value.

## Empowerment is about learning

Unless there is freedom for individuals at all levels to learn and develop, the empowered culture will never arrive. Part of learning is people stretching beyond their zones of comfort and trying new skills. If a person stands still and operates within prescribed roles and functions, they have no opportunity to take 'thoughtful risks'. Taking risks helps develop confidence to look at new ways of learning. Most companies discourage staff from taking risks and define their roles in terms of conducting tasks in an ordained manner. This has to be rejected in re-engineered organisations, in which people contribute positively to a process.

**'Re-engineering cannot work in organisations which prescribe jobs as tasks.'**

It is impossible to re-engineer organisations into process flows and not challenge the role that people perform. As the focus on process is expanded, people move away from contributing to discrete functional activities and adopt new ways of working which rejects the old demarcation lines and job descriptions. To operate in this environment requires people to learn beyond their current 'discrete and specific functional tasks' and operate more flexibly. This transition can be stressful and anxiety provoking. A good guide to help managers understand this process is:

**'Does the change to a person's role diminish or increase self esteem?'**

If it diminishes and puts the person at potential disadvantage, the learning opportunity must be driven in such a way that the person can only succeed. This is fundamentally the role of the manager: to coach and promote genuine self esteem within staff.

## Freedom not abdication

An empowered business requires a choice on the part of managers to give their people freedom of movement and to think for themselves. Empowerment is not abdication where the manager gives up all form of guidance and control, leaving staff to fend for themselves and develop by chance. Empowerment is about the manager changing his dominant role from one of controlling activities of others to that of coaching and guiding them to develop their own abilities to best serve the business, their colleagues and themselves.

## Empowerment – not understood

Empowerment is best illustrated by the degree to which control over staff is replaced by trust. Moving from a 'control' culture to one of 'trust' does not happen overnight and will never happen if the favourable change is not driven at two levels: management and the managed.

Empowerment can be just as challenging for the manager as for staff – especially in organisations where staff are still functionally organised.

## Unless it starts from the top, it's going nowhere

As with all change initiatives, if is practised from the top down there is every likelihood it will work. But empowerment will never happen in a structure in which the manager openly empowers staff to perform their work. Empowerment cannot be bestowed on one person by another – it is a state of being, a climate which allows people to use their own power and knowledge. It will never reside in organisations where managers evaluate and decide how people will pursue their role because 'over control' takes away personal choice.

People already have power through knowledge and motivation. Empowerment is letting this power flow into the business.

## Where does empowerment start?

It starts with adopting an open book approach to the business. Open book management is based upon sharing that which affects people and the organisation. It is an approach to disclose information which previously was restricted, for whatever reason, to a select strata or group. Usually, the information we are talking about goes far beyond the profit and loss account and balance sheet, although this is a good place to start. It is founded upon the premise that people make the best decisions based on the information which is available to them at the time. By providing information in user friendly language tailored to the audience means people will then be able to make more informed decisions.

## Information sharing and the open book

Understanding business information goes beyond learning to understand annual reports, assets and liabilities. It is a means whereby information can be exposed to the people who use their experience to help them make more informed, better quality decisions which will be advantageous for the business. It is based upon the idea that people seek responsibility and enhancement and will generate wisdom for improved performance. This is where the term the 'learning organisation' applies. People are the embodiment of the culture of the business and if conditions permit, the organisation will learn and grow wise. But only if the right conditions are created for wisdom to evolve.

The power of the learning organisation is that people can be trained in all manner of techniques and approaches to apply their natural curiosity and contribution to make things better. That when staff believe they can influence events, after careful analysis, discussion and debate, they will contribute in a significant manner.

All businesses could function and prosper with this approach because they would have a continuous stream of ideas waiting to be implemented.

An empowered business is where there are good ideas for improvement waiting to be implemented by managers who spend time developing and coaching their people, rather than measuring and controlling processes.

Who develops the ideas? Staff other than managers, because they know what works and what does not. People who do the work are closest to the problems and the process and understand the complex interplay of cause effect factors. Those who work the process have much more expertise than those who manage it. Their ideas, after testing and discussion in a team environment, will, when implemented, work well and will further promote continuous improvement.

A client told me he had one goal when introducing culture change into his law firm:

> **'I want my people who leave work on a Friday evening to say to themselves – damn, it's two more days before I can get back into the office.'**

This comment reflected his desire to create an environment where people would love to contribute and really make a difference rather than an unhealthy desire and imbalance towards work as the only life interest. It certainly reflects my view that, in order to enjoy work, we should do as much as we can to make it a stimulating and valuable experience for everyone. If everyone in a business holds that belief, it will happen very quickly. The belief will take hold in management circles and the empowered culture will mushroom.

## Flat structures

Having too many layers of management will disempower staff to contribute, especially when people in positions of power have rigid structures with firm spans of control. Many years ago Grinocious, a mathematician, said it was impossible to manage and control the activities of more than six to eight people. He based his ideas on the number of communication channels that could be set up with the team and his direct reports. What nonsense. Based upon that concept, most businesses would require many levels of management. The more levels of management there are, the more isolated the top people are from what is going on at the bottom.

The more layers there are, the more the top team are cocooned from the reality of service delivery and the machinations which drive a business. There are no rules for spans of control in an role or job. A good friend and a vice president of a major global financial services business states it clearly:

"It doesn't matter how many people report to you. It's only the difficult ones you have to manage."

If you have been doing your job properly, developing your people, building a team, facilitating progress and setting a firm example, you will not have difficulty managing people. Your people will be managing themselves.

Reassessed structures should be firmly built around the strategy the business is pursuing. The strategy will reflect processes which have been totally re-engineered to focus almost entirely on the external customer.

## Staff as strategists

Staff who support and work the core processes should play a major part in formulating strategy. They interact most with the internal customer chain and have their part to play in a bottom-up strategy implementation process. When disclosing information about potential for the business, new products and markets, key threats and opportunities as well as core vulnerabilities, the average staff member will want to contribute. Few people go to work just to do a job or perform activities by rote. That is the way they will behave sometimes because that is a result of how they are managed. If the focus is on cost reduction in a department and on applying rigid cost control, you can hardly give your people a hard time for not concentrating on quality and customer care.

Some companies have a long route ahead before they can create a truly empowered business. But the options for change are many and obvious.

## Vertical and horizontal loading

There are many routes to help ease empowerment into a business. They can start at fairly modest levels before moving to one of the ideals of self directed work teams. This starts with completely redesigning the role of people or their jobs. Historically, jobs and their scope of responsibility and required skills have been determined by strict specialisation of labour. The result was low job responsibility with highly repetitive jobs resulting in high labour turnover and low job satisfaction. The design of jobs was undoubtedly heavily influenced by the dominant mass production technology. The disadvantages of designing jobs were obvious and the only advantages were focused upon cost. In those days and in those types of businesses there was little interest in maximising the potential of their people. Interest was purely on utilising people as mere tools in the process of task completion.

As a more human approach to managing people was adopted we found that more and more businesses were expanding the scope of jobs both horizontally and vertically. By way of example, the job scope could be expanded horizontally by increasing or enlarging the nature of the tasks – at the same intellectual level; or increasing the variety of tasks performed through job rotation. Rather than doing one boring job all day, the individual worker would perform several boring, repetitive jobs in sequence. This attempt to redesign jobs was relatively unsuccessful in many areas because the nature of the person's role did not change. Vertical loading would see many job holders significantly improving performance. The reason? That the nature of the job was enriched by giving vertical responsibility and may have involved significant decision-making. It seemed, in those days, that companies or organisations were based on classical lines, with strict demarcation between those who controlled processes and those who did the work.

A humanistic approach to job design focuses on the person and their skills as well as the environment, ecology, health and safety, the technology employed and the nature of the work. Psychological factors now play a part in helping to design the workplace for the requirements of the individual and the organisation.

Empowerment takes this a stage further because it goes beyond physical, humanistic and environmental considerations to the psychological and spiritual. Empowerment is concerned with tapping the essence of man and using the organisation as a laboratory for thoughtful experimentation. People understand the contribution they can make and will work together contributing ideas and making decisions based not on seniority, but on knowledge of the task or process. This involves learning from others and providing opportunities for enhancement personally and in a team. This I see as spiritual development or, as Abraham Maslow would have depicted it, the pinnacle of existence or self actualisation, as in his needs hierarchy. Whether this is ever achieved is of immense interest. It does not matter if you get there because the journey itself will be worthwhile. But if you achieve even 70% of this vision, the results for your business will be enormous.

## Wot! no managers – self directed work teams

If organisations can achieve this degree of empowerment (and I believe many have) what need is there for managers? Are they required at all? Perhaps we will be organised more on the lines of small numbers of staff focused upon technical input. Team members would be equally skilled in communicating their specialism, with the vast majority of what we call managers occupying the role of coaches, team leaders and facilitators. They would be solely committed to helping others achieve results, helping them master the process of change.

Many organisations are organised around self directed work teams. Much of this system stems from research into the Volvo experiment in Sweden, and the Saab Scandia experience, where small groups were set up to assemble vehicles. Quality improved substantially and the outcome for staff was a high degree of job satisfaction, particularly as jobs had been redesigned around more humanistic variables than cost or technology. Self directed teams are much further along this continuum of empowerment but can start off being quite structured and focused.

An experience in a process flow chemical industry convinced me that it can work well. Much of this work has been applied in large financial services businesses where re-engineered processes are now managed by teams rather than managers.

In this case, the chemical company applied a five-shift system. Each production area, of which there were three, had its own shift rota, shift foreman for each shift and one manager. The manager would oversee things between nine and five while each shift foreman ran things around the continental five shift system.

Because of competitive pressures, the business had to improve quality, reduce delivery hold-ups, improve customer service, reduce costs associated with poor quality and make more productive use of the management team liaising with other plants around the world.

Clearly, the role of the management team would have to change from managing and controlling individual shift foremen and five-shift teams, to working more strategically with the focus of creating a culture of continuous improvement. To take on more of the manager's role, foremen would have to learn new skills and drive ideas on quality improvement. This required each foremen to develop an understanding beyond his own functional area.

At that time, foremen started their cross-training with the purpose of being competent to manage any shift in any area. This further pushed responsibility down to the work team to organise recording of production, quality control, overtime, holiday cover and all the activities traditionally managed by others.

Interest was focused on the whole process, right across the plant, not just a discrete manufacturing area. The teams developed cross-functional training and took on the role of self-managed groups. Five years later, work in the chemical plant is completely revolutionised. Foremen no longer exist – they have been replaced by team coaches devoting all their time to researching training needs. Those who used to be managed in work teams are completely cross-trained in all areas, including health and safety.

Granted there are fewer staff – mostly due to natural attrition – but the plant is still in operation as major profit centre. If old work practices had not changed, the way work was organised would have made the plant uncompetitive. Without doubt it would have closed years ago with many redundancies in an area in which unemployment is extremely high.

## Pressure and drive for change

Re-engineering around self managed groups changed the culture and made it far more effective and team oriented. Production staff regularly visit customers and suppliers to help them work through problems with change and quality improvement.

Several businesses currently are pursuing a similar theme. Idealistically, it would be more desirable to 'pull' people through the process at their own pace. But real world competitive pressures sometimes force companies and businesses to 'push' the process in less than desirable time frames. If there was not a need to change and improve, the culture may have remained the same. But when we have pressures to improve quality, reduce cycle times, improve customer focus and take on the perspective and profile of six sigma companies, change is seen as a necessity.

## Preparing for empowerment

A thorough review of the structure of the business is required. You have to structure for change. If the goal is empowerment, with all the benefits which accrue, you cannot develop a flexible organisation with captains and lieutenants of industry defending their functional silos. You must structure for change.

## Summary and bullet points

Empowerment is the means to achieve culture change and the end goal. It requires substantial rethinking about the role of managers and about re-engineering processes and relationships. The goal is a learning organisation committed to implementing best practice faster than competitors. With that goal in mind, the end result is security for the business and for staff.

- Empowerment is a greatly overused and misunderstood term.

- Empowerment and delegation are a million miles apart.

- You can't empower other people. They have to take the power of their knowledge and apply it themselves.

- You can't empower people but you can create the climate in which empowerment will take place.

- Empowerment is not abdication.

- You have to prepare for an empowering culture.

- Define broad boundaries within which people can operate. These boundaries must be flexible, allowing movement in and out of personal 'comfort zones'.

- Agree key result areas and desired outcomes for roles. Reject job descriptions as too prescriptive in focus and restrictive in actions.

- Change the role of the job, even the job title, to promote self esteem.

- Reconsider job titles, teams and departments to project a realistic but positive and active role rather than a description of a task.

- Do anything to make people feel better about the role that they play. If they feel better, their contribution will be more significant.

- Learning is critical when empowering staff. If you expect them to take on more responsibility, they have got to understand the breadth and impact of the work they are due to control.

- Learning cannot happen without making mistakes. From the 3% of failures comes the 99% of success.

- Learning requires risk taking. Taking thoughtful risks should be rewarded.

- You can't re-engineer a business with minimal commitment to empowerment.

- If changing a person's role increases his self esteem, do it. It will certainly increase his contribution.

- Empowerment is rejecting the mentality of over-control and replacing it with trust.

- Open book management is a good way to start the empowering process.

- There is no alternative – it has to start top down.

- Empowerment can't be given. People have to be prepared to take the power.

- Share information, listen to your people, implement their ideas. This reinforces your trust in them.

- Flat structures promote free transfer of information and ideas.

- Forget pre-ordained spans of control. You should only manage difficult people.

- Redesign jobs around human needs.

- Vertically load jobs to add to job satisfaction and scope.

- Understand that the role of self directed work teams replaces the traditional over-controlling view of management.

- Prepare the culture for empowerment by structuring for change.

*Chapter 12:*

# Managing performance

If an organisation has made the effort to realign culture to reflect its mission, if it has worked through the key issues from clarifying values and linking them to expected managerial behaviours, related behaviours to core competencies, and has worked on motivational and leadership issues, it must sustain the improvement drive through managing performance. Traditionally, this area is neglected in the typical organisation. Recipients of poor performance assessment practice argue that rewards are often based on scant performance information; the whole motivational calculus is thrown into disarray. In terms of sustaining a consistent, performance-driven business, this is probably one of the most important issues for management teams .

It is equally important to manage the performance of poor as well as good, performers. Many organisations fail to deal with significant performance issues.

**'Colleagues who are HR directors highlight that on average 10 to 25% of employees can be classed as poor performers.'**

This is a serious issue, a reflection of how people are managed and led. A director in the voluntary sector told me that performance issues in his organisation (sports coaching) were ignored because of difficulties with appraising and assessing volunteers. This is understandable when there is no formal, legal, relationship between manager and managed. But there is no excuse when this happens in a commercial business setting.

Managing the performance of others is a major issue determined by the skills and abilities of those who manage. This is just as true in bureaucracies in the private sector as it is in the public sector.

**149**

Poor management of poor performance has a major impact on the morale of a business and its performance. Worse still, when managers fail to take action to resolve performance issues, the morale of all in the area or location is affected. Where issues are left to fester and poor performers are retained, there is a huge negative effect on the motivation, morale, team working and, ultimately, customer satisfaction.

## A case in managing performance

Featured in this short case is a division of a leading finance house which provides point of sale finance to the motor trade, and which has managed change in turbulent times. With high interest rates in the late 80s, and increasing customer defaults continuing into the mid 90s, this company has experienced great change in the way it does business. If the company had not focused upon creating a culture of performance improvement, market share would have been lost. Focusing efforts in this way investing in technology and restructuring the company helped to consolidate its business and reap further rewards.

Historically, the company had contemplated the Total Quality route. After employing different groups of consultants, whose reports suggested that cultural change was required, they decided to develop what some senior staff considered a high-risk option: strike at the very fabric of the organisation by changing the style of managers, starting at the very top.

Over two years the drive for cultural change achieved a great deal. Managers attended cultural change workshops, each based on sound action learning principles. Between each workshop, they worked on changing aspects of behaviour and style to achieve a positive impact on their part.

A manager in charge of a small unit would be responsible for changing that part of the culture. The principles for change were founded on six core values to which the board had committed. Each manager was a change agent, forging his or her efforts to promote a vibrant culture in which employees felt empowered to challenge, change and improve.

## Changing behaviour

All senior staff including board members, operational directors and those managing branches and headquarters functions, developed measurable action plans for change. Attention was focused upon changing behaviour. All areas were progressing in some way. Success was evident in many .

Examples of success included:

- 100% staff attendance at monthly communication meetings at all locations. Staff volunteered to chair communication meetings and developed their own agenda for discussion. This was a reversal of practice. Managers were no longer seen as the only force in managing meetings, nor were they the 'font of knowledge' when it came to suggesting ideas to promote better customer service.

- Many meetings were geared towards 'localised strategic planning'. Each branch office, employing on average, 20 people, created its own strategic plan, including target sales and measures to assess performance. New customers were targeted and information was displayed to ensure everyone was aware of objectives.

- Ideas for change were implemented. Some locations adopted a modified approach to quality improvement, with promises from managers that 80% of improvements would be implemented within three months. The majority of managers who made this commitment kept it.

## Culture change and market reality

The effect of cultural change was positive with a focus on improvement, communication and working in teams. Savings in rework activities were also realised.

However, the culture was not yet strong enough to take the effort further and make the self-perpetuating gains associated with continuous improvement. The company was still experiencing increasing debts caused by poor quality underwriting. This resulted in customer defaults – a major threat to the business. Much of the 'soft' side of the culture was in place but there was still a need to refocus the attention of all employees.

Without the cultural change initiative, focusing on 'performance improvement', the means of measuring performance and value added would not be realised.

## Ignoring poor performance

During training workshops, poor control and poor management of people was evident. Many 'people management' issues were being deliberately ignored. For this reason, we devised a two-day performance management workshop which focused on achieving tangible results. Everyone who managed staff, over 200 managers and supervisors, attended the sessions. The highly interactive workshops focused on changing individual behaviour. At the end, each participant completed an action plan for implementation within their work area.

To guarantee individual involvement and contribution, attendance at each workshop was limited to eight. Over the two days the workshop was held, participants took part in these activities:

- Managers studied performance management cases and feedback, giving recommended courses of action.

- They took part in four monitored role-plays, each lasting 30 minutes. Feedback was invited after each role play. Each manager played the role of appraiser and appraisee on two occasions, with direct and honest feedback from the appraisee and others attending the exercise.

- Self assessment questionnaires on values and attitudes had the ultimate purpose of radically improving the way in which performance of staff was managed.

## Managing difficult people

While trying to change culture, emphasis should be directed towards changing the way managers think and, consequently, behave. In many sessions, the issue of managing difficult people arose. It appeared that too many managers managed and, unwittingly, encouraged poor performance.

Managers recounted tales of bloody-minded individuals who would not change. They also talked of how difficult it was to remove them from the structure. In fact, this became such an over-riding concern that I spent a lot of time with human resources staff responsible for administering the current performance management process. I was shocked by the research. On investigation, it became clear that line managers were the real problem – they were failing to take responsibility and achieve results through their people.

Facts about the practice of performance management:

- More than 50% of appraisals over six months late.

- Many staff appraisals were more than 6 months late.

- Assessments were completed in word but not in deed – staff were often told to sign their assessment without recourse to discussion on improving performance.

- Some senior managers had not been appraised in seven years.

- Some assessments were completed as a result of constant harassment by human resources.

- Performance management was seen as a human resource, not a line management, responsibility.

Many appraisals were done 'to' rather than 'with' people. The 'sign here' syndrome was much in evidence. It became apparent that performance assessment did not happen. Ask yourself how many issues are unresolved in your own business.

## Performance management does not work in most organisations.

A measure to assess the effective management of people is to assess the value and effectiveness of assessment systems.

Very few companies have performance management systems that work. There is usually nothing wrong with the system or procedure – one is very similar to another. Neither does the paperwork, or documentation which supports such systems, vary a great deal. What is important is the inter-personal process. The process of performance management is neglected because it is perceived as stressful and difficult to manage. Not necessarily for the person receiving the assessment – but for the person conducting it.

Research suggests that most managers tend to concentrate on the tangible aspects of performance appraisal, focusing on structure, systems and documentation. What makes a performance management system work is managing the process, not filling in countless forms.

Unfortunately, people are not trained to manage the process because this requires them to move beyond their comfort zones. Instead, they rely on the formal process and guidance on how to complete documentation. This formal process ends when they send assessments to the personnel or human resources department. We found that, unless HR questioned the assessment, the line manager would continue working with sub-standard performers without taking the required action. In fact, HR would be blamed for not dealing with the issue. This is still prevalent in far too many businesses. The issue is one for line management; passing the buck to HR does not work. HR is the post box where information is stored. The line manager is there to manage on a day-to-day basis.

## The process of performance management

The process involves interacting with each member of your staff, creating a climate of mutual trust (this is not a one day event), listening, advising, being honest, counselling, giving praise, giving bad news (hardly ever), following up and meeting agreements, setting joint objectives (not imposing theirs) and winning the commitment and ownership of the appraisee to contribute more to the business.

## Managing the process

Research in the quoted organisation suggested that less than 50% of appraisals were completed on time. Research also showed that, of 950 people employed, only three were on any form of disciplinary action or counselling. This was amazing, suggesting that the company had no problems with staff. For an organisation with, apparently, such good or above average performers, overall company results were disappointing.

In reality, the company tolerated poor performance and did little to eradicate it. There were few instances of people being fired. Job security was almost 100%. I discovered later that too many managers encouraged poor performance by default. Their inaction created a 'don't care if you do, don't care if you don't' environment where work was perceived as a 9-5 activity and where there was little pressure for any improvement.

Most managers would not agree there were performance problems. But in reality they shared all sorts of difficulties, such as not being able to give staff bad news. They were adamant that they were 'macho managers'. Evidence suggested they avoided dealing with critical issues and portrayed a 'couldn't care less attitude'.

At the start of training sessions, participants claimed they did not have a problem with appraisal, but the truth emerged. Most admitted to experiencing a great deal of stress when conducting assessments in real life. Managers said they did not know how to do it. They soon came to understand it was not a technical process which could be learned by rote. Because the process was open ended, it required planning and often involved the transmission of bad as well as good news – a process many managers went to great lengths to avoid.

Examples of 'avoidance' behaviour:

- Failing to conduct the assessment. The manager completing the appraisal forms, and requesting a signature, indicated little or no discussion coming from the person who had been interviewed.

- Examples of duplicating the assessment from the previous year. (Phoning personnel department for a copy of the previous year's appraisal, copying and submitting the same information.)

- Some examples of conducting assessments quickly in a public place, for example airports and wine bars.

- Focusing almost exclusively on technical, rather than management, issues.

## Macho management

One manager was quite upset when it was mentioned that his excellent salary, prestige car and mortgage subsidy was paid in return for managing people. He was under the mistaken belief that he was paid for his technical ability to underwrite financial deals.

Our educational programme focused on the manager as change agent and builder of teams. We came to the conclusion that too many companies focus on the technical expertise of their senior staff rather than on their ability to achieve results through others. Our intervention was to focus upon the line manager as change agent.

# Competing for a scarce resource: people

If organisations are to survive, there has to be recognition that people are their most valuable and creative resource. We must also understand the impact of the demographic downturn – smaller numbers of bright young people coming on the market. The implication is that companies are competing for an increasingly scarce resource. Availability of fewer good quality people suggests it is a sellers' market.

This means that companies will have to provide an excellent working environment and development for its people. Rewards and recognition must be based on equitable assessment and progression.

News that companies have a poor reputation or culture will spread, discouraging 'bright people' from entering the business and 'losing the best' to organisations which project the best in people assessment and progression.

# Rosie and the canal incident

A good example of a manager not taking responsibility for managing others was referred to as the 'canal incident.' Rosie, who had been employed for 15 years, had an attendance problem. Of an annual 210 working days, was absent for approximately 30, excluding holiday entitlement.

Her reasons were mainly sickness. Statutory sick pay absence records were submitted with the following reasons for non-attendance. Note that reasons were never challenged.

As well as 20 days for illnesses such as stomach bugs, colds, viral infections, back pain, stomach cramps and toothache, I observed the following problems:

| | |
|---|---|
| Jellylegged | Two days |
| Bad head and sweating | Three days |
| Bitten by a hen | Two days |
| Vindalood | One day |
| Fell in canal | Two days |

To make matters worse, Rosie had asked for two days' absence, without pay, because her horse would be giving birth.

Something was wrong. Perhaps these incidents were genuine, but Rosie's behaviour was unacceptable. What's more, it had not been questioned by her line manager. Although the excuses created a great deal of mirth and hilarity in the training workshop (anonymity was strictly preserved) the serious question was: why was this behaviour not questioned? Because the manager could not confront, be honest, create an open climate and ultimately could not convey bad news.

## Failing to be honest

The above instance, although extreme, is the norm rather than the exception.

Rosie's behaviour was clearly creating problems. The apparent acceptance of her behaviour by her manager was tantamount to defining the acceptable standard of behaviour for everybody in the office. Understandably, morale was low. Others thought they were being treated poorly by having to cover for their colleague's constant absence. There was a great deal of resentment within the work group.

Because behaviour had not been questioned, problems with morale were created. What eventually evolved in the work groups was an attitude that it was okay to take a few days off. Why not? Rosie did.

Others believed her approach to work was an acceptable standard of performance. The manager said he was powerless – he could do nothing. Instead, he blamed human resources and their (apparent) complicated disciplinary process. He suggested bureaucracy created too much of a problem for getting rid of poor performers.

On investigation, I found that the manager had been told to fill out a short report. This information would enable appropriate action to be taken. The report was never received and was not chased up. The manager did not want to document the case, which may mean he would have to institute and manage the disciplinary process locally. He did not wish to be unpopular.

## Managing poor performance

The 'canal incident' is not unusual. It is probably a common problem in many companies. Managers seem to have a block about giving bad news because they cannot handle the emotions of others.

# Managers cannot handle emotion

Even when they tell someone their staff are under-performing, many executives have difficulty managing the ensuing conflict. Bad news has to be discussed. It cannot be managed through a door. It cannot be transmitted and resolved by a memo. It has to be discussed eyeball to eyeball. It has to be honest and clean.

Managers often fail to face reality. Their poor performance creates situations where staff fail to meet requirements. Many let down staff by over-promising and under-delivering. Managers have to be prepared to listen critically to what staff think of them. If a member of staff fails, does the failure occur because his manager has failed to develop, coach, train, counsel and set joint goals? Or is he, the managed, poor material? The former is usually the case.

In most companies a poorly branded version of culture change is not always the solution to problem-solving. Many problems continue after companies have been sold the latest quick fix. Because the company has failed to change the culture, it is left with the original problem – it cannot get the most from its people. The main reason is often that managers are ill-equipped to achieve results through others.

### Solution = leadership

The solution for these companies is train the hell out of managers, with one clear intention: lead, lead, lead.

Culture change unearths the practices in many organisations. These practices can remain unaddressed unless the management and leadership issues are resolved.

# The acid test

To assess the extent to which a management group deals with the key issues of failing to manage poor performers, apply this test. Ask managers what they would do if they ran their own business and employed the staff they currently manage. Continue the story. If things go well for the company, the owner will become wealthy and may sell his business for considerable gain. However, if business performance declines, he may risk personal financial failure – losing all. Now the crunch question:

**"If your business comprised the people you currently manage, what percentage would you retain?"**

Interestingly, the average figure was 70%, with variations down to as little as 50%. This indicates that managers would manage differently and adopt different standards if the business was their own. Obviously, this is the focus of serious debate about management commitment and loyalty to the company. This is striking at the very heart of the fabric of the organisation.

I put the same question to two levels of management in the same business unit. On average, the senior of the two managers suggested a higher percentage for retention than his or her junior colleague, indicating that the junior manager would make more changes or dismissals. Sometimes the variation was considerable. This suggested that the management group failed to discuss the real people issues within their own business unit. This is probably the most critical issue concerning cultural change. Another issue is that junior management often to fail to tell their immediate boss about 'problem cases'. One can only make assumptions as to why this occurs.

## Human resources have no responsibility for performance management

The human resources department should be no more than a mail box for performance appraisal documentation. They play no part in the living breathing reality of appraisal and assessment. HR are responsible for designing the system and procedure (together with line management) collating, administering and recording the process, processes training when requested, and providing legal and other support.

Line management is fully responsible for making the system 'live and breathe.' If the performance management system does not work, it is because managers do not want it to work. If companies do not have an effective succession plan it is because line managers do not want one. If companies are manned by poor performers, it is because line managers want it that way.

## Most organisations employ 10% to 30% poor performers

My belief is that most successful organisations are lucky that not more than seven to ten percent of the workforce are poor performers. Most companies over-employ poor performers – anywhere between 10% to 30% of all staff. I am concerned that this percentage can remain constant even after the introduction of culture change. This is because too many change efforts concentrate on systems and procedural issues rather than redesigning the fabric of the organisation. Cultural change is about creating powerful leaders rather than highly-paid technical managers who cannot develop a team or motivate people.

## Setting performance standards

It comes as no surprise that performance standards are conspicuous by their absence. Targets and key performance measures are most evident in manufacturing companies or in sales environments. It is of concern that, in too many cases, what people do at work reflects their preference rather than their job description.

I have never been in favour of job descriptions because they create demarcation lines and stifle individual creativity and hinder flexibility. However, I feel that commitment should be focused upon key result areas.

I constantly find that staff are very busy but add little value to the process in which they are key. For instance, in the company quoted earlier, account managers who regularly visit dealers spend too much time collecting and delivering documentation rather than adding value. It is easier to be visible than to invest in value creation.

In order to reverse this trend, key dealers were allocated to individual account managers and new performance measures were instituted. Call plans were created and adhered to. Furthermore, this trend was continued with administrative staff in all business units. Previously, experience had dictated a 'feel' for performance. Now, objective measures were in place. There were times set for loading documents into the computer system, telephone collection calls to defaulters, and times agreed for processing work. Generally the new measures were accepted.

In one location the manager had set targets for his staff and was surprised to find that, on average, they exceeded the performance measure by 30%. This strengthened the cultural view that staff should be responsible for setting their own agreed performance standards.

## Learning to manage performance

Very little inter-personal skills training had been administered before the cultural change initiative. Now, after a two-day workshop, managers and supervisors felt more in control of the 'process' of managing. They found that the stress experienced before the assessment had diminished, partly due to the preparation they now complete in order to do a good job. The view expressed by some participants was that preparation they put into role plays far exceeded preparation for real life.

Just because manager and managed come into contact every day, it should not be assumed that the manager understands the key issues to be discussed in the assessment. Real performance assessment requires preparation by both parties. Parameters have to be set prior to formal meetings and a potential agenda of key issues discussed. Managers have been trained not to debate and discuss issues with people who have not prepared and who are not taking the process seriously. The 'process' is jointly owned by both parties. Assessment and objective setting is not to be imposed and 'done to' but 'with' the person being assessed.

Training focused on the process of performance enhancement. No reference was made to completion of documents. The focus was on agreeing five key result areas and agreeing three-month targets for continued discussion. It was agreed during the training workshops that each member of staff should have a formal opportunity to move through the performance enhancement process every three months.

As key result measures, and performance indicators became visible, the process became easier and less time-consuming. Some managers thought the three-monthly appraisal was too time-consuming. To convince them of its value, they were presented with an outline of the managerial job, not to do technical things but to ensure that people were managed. I found in many instances that too many managers were appraising all staff in the business unit and taking responsibility away from supervisors. I strongly discouraged this trend and now ensure that any manager or supervisor takes full responsibility to assess only his or her direct reports.

I also found that managers spend an inordinate amount of time talking during these assessments. In most sessions the rule was to minimise talking and question-asking to 10% of total time. Using CCTV, I ascertained that too many managers answer their own questions and never spend enough time listening. This feedback helped to change their behaviour.

## Action planning and change

I would not let managers leave a session without committing themselves to action. Most action plans focused on speaking less and avoiding the development of an attitude prior to the interview, thus creating a self-fulfilling story. On the tangible side, most committed to identifying, experimenting with and setting up key result areas in all aspects of the job, rather than just the technical issues.

## Summary and bullet points

This extremely successful process is applicable to most. Many of the non-performers have been identified and a large number have left the company. Following coaching by line managers, those who had been performing poorly are now living up to the standard expected. Without this change in behaviour, it is unlikely that the company would be as successful as it is today. This makes us wonder how often people need clear guidance to enable them to contribute.

More time is now devoted to value added activities. There are no time fillers. People's preferences have given way to company targets.

The culture is more positive. People know what is expected of them. No assumptions are made about what people do.

If there is confusion about work output and quality, parameters for performance measurement can best be set by the person who does the job, in liaison with his or her line manager.

In this company, the cultural change drive has had ups and downs. This is how it happens in practice. Industry does not always explain what has worked in culture change and what has not. But I am certain that this one initiative did much to put the company in the fast lane, in spite of pressures in the industry. The drive has been successful because it has touched and influenced the the way people are managed.

What I learned from the intervention is that cultural change takes time and that if such a drive fails to influence what people do on a day-to-day level, it most certainly has been flavour of the month.

• What's the point of a strong culture if you fail to guide and manage performance?

• The impact of not dealing with poor staff performance can have a dire effect on group morale.

• It's my experience that managers are too embarrassed to thank and praise people for a job well done and are afraid to deal with poor performers.

- It is easy to change the behaviour of others in the management group. Just do what you want them to do and do it tirelessly.

- There are few recorded cases of managers and leaders being over-trained to conduct their role of managing the performance of others.

- If you want others to change it may not be a bad idea to find out how others rate your behaviour. Try asking them 'how am I doing?'

- Performance management does not always work in large organisations because it requires managers to take issues right through the organisational hierarchy.

- Remember, HR will not solve your man-management problems. But they will support you in skills and help with policy. You are paid to manage your people.

- Most will not admit to having difficulty with managing performance and appraising at regular intervals.

- Managers cannot always handle emotion – especially their own – when they give bad news.

- A great number of issues in man-management are avoided.

- The cornerstone of effective performance assessment is mutual trust.

- If your business was your own, what percentage of the people you currently manage would you retain?

- Most organisations over-employ poor performers to the tune of 10% to 30%.

- Set challenging performance standards. And give those who do the job equal part in the process.

*Chapter 13:*

# Re-engineering a strong customer focus

When revising and redesigning a business culture there is a strong requirement to consider the organisation's core constituents. Much of this book has been written to focus upon maximising the contribution of the people who drive the business. However, an organisation totally focused on its staff to the exclusion of external customers would be nonsensical. In previous sections it has been assumed that the reason for existence of the business is to meet the need of customers or consumers. But still too few businesses focus their attention on the customer; the purpose of this chapter is to focus on the customer as the *raison d'être* for any organisation.

## Customer service benefits

In an environment in which customer choice is rapidly increasing, organisations which create a powerful customer-focused infrastructure will retain customers.

> **'Many are still not aware that the average business loses as much as 80% of its customer base every five years. And it costs five times as much to win the support of a new customer than retain an existing one.'**

This is especially the case in the service sector where choice is high. There are protected industries and monopoly providers where the risk is not so tough, but they are still at risk in the medium term. Companies which consider their customer base not at risk need urgently to create barriers to entry. There is no such thing as a safe market.

Customer charters have largely focused the attention of those in the public sector or those who are in a monopoly position and sliding charges or fines penalise many service providers. But the time will come when adherence to anything less than 100% customer delight will lead to significant fall in demand for any organisation's services.

Companies and organisations which have not yet focused upon improving customer service face a shaky future. Some years ago, I was attracted to Richard Whiteley's research into customer service. Richard is one of the key motivators behind The Forum Corporation, a US consultancy promoting customer service strategy. I was impressed by their research which suggested that as many as 96% of corporate problems were not disclosed to the top team of any business. Not all these problems are related to direct facing customer contact, but any problem will impact on the customer eventually. I was interested in this work because it dovetailed with my view that managers do not always understand how the dynamics operate within their own business culture.

## The iceberg of ignorance

To illustrate this point, I was holding a discussion in an open workshop on change skills. People were talking about what was considered 'acceptable quality levels' (AQLs) in their business. Delegates from an insurance business and the public sector quoted a desired AQL or non-conformance rate of being maintained at 10% to 15%. This meant a failure rate as high as 10% to 15% of variable costs like salaries and was considered a respectable norm. This implied that only 85% to 90% of work processed was right first time. Many at the workshop found this unacceptable.

This was like saying it was perfectly acceptable that the norm of 10% to 15% of work would have to be reworked or reprocessed. In response to the question of who pays for this rework or the non-conformances that have to be processed again, the answer was that this charge would usually be included and accepted in normal operating costs. A shocking response!

In the real world, it isn't the company that underwrites this cost — it is the customer. The customer pays for all errors and omissions created by the service provider. Like it or not, they have a choice to seek other suppliers.

## Customers dictating the price of components

Some years ago, I worked with a large business producing catalytic converters and exhaust or muffler systems for cars. A Japanese manufacturer, keen to purchase components from this automotive supplier, sent in a team of people to inspect the production process. Their conclusion was that the cost of manufacture was greatly enhanced because of high failure rates; this automatically bumped the price of the finished component to the customer by as much as 30%. After the 'cost estimators' had researched into the company, their response to the supplier was simple: "If you want our custom, engage in a TQ and quality assurance programme immediately."

They envisaged the supplier reducing unnecessary manufacturing costs by 20% within three years. Their projections, and the price that they would be willing to pay over a three year period, was much lower than the price currently demanded. The Japanese car manufacturer understood they were paying for the inefficiencies of their suppliers. The company's 'cost estimators' took good care to ensure they always got value for money from all suppliers.

Much of what the cost estimators based their judgement on was unknown to the plant management team or the top team. This illustrates that the 'iceberg of ignorance' is a big issue in some businesses.

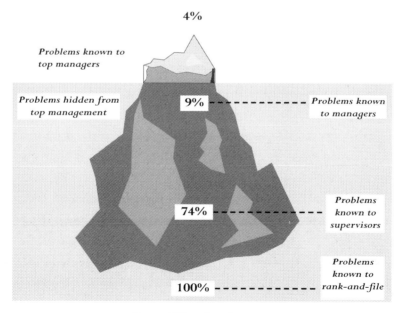

Diagram 7. The iceberg of ignorance

You might want to ask yourself the following questions, which ultimately impact on customer service:

- **What problems are the top management group unaware of? How could they impact negatively on customer relations?**

- **What is the current state of knowledge on the three key customer challenges facing your business? What are you doing to resolve them?**

Working on these key issues will ensure that the organisation is becoming more customer focused. They should be central to any change initiative.

## Re-engineer all processes to become customer focused

Infrastructure is incredibly important. It is vital to look at all processes which underpin service delivery as requiring to be customer-focused. Many organisations are not. Processes are often organised around tasks which are completed by departments and functions. Thus the order entry process is owned by the sales function; customer relations by marketing; invoicing by finance; delivery, manufacture and distribution by production. Organised this way, on classical lines, the average organisation will never be able to deliver error-free service on time. Examining traditional working around functions highlights major gulfs between departmental silos, breakdowns in communication, poor response to customer enquiries and a disjointed view on optimising customer service.

Customer service should be error-free, speedy, seamless and organised and driven by people who understand the process from start to finish. It is no good having a multitude of staff and managers contacting, and communicating with, the customer to resolve problems in an isolated fashion — it confuses the customer.

Recently, while working with a major company, I was shocked to find that a customer in the Far East had been visited in the same week by four staff members of the supplying company. One was from technical services, to advise on manufacturing issues; one was from sales, for orders and new product development; one from finance, discussing new billing agreements and how it would affect their joint venture activities; and an IT specialist, discussing development of joint systems. Each person, unaware of the presence of their colleagues, demonstrated a complete focus on functional issues.

The customer was furious that four people travelled from the UK, in uncoordinated fashion, taking up precious time of his staff. What really displeased this customer was that the trips were not coordinated and the associated cost was ultimately borne by him. This uncoordinated effort is not uncommon in businesses which are organised on traditional, functional lines.

Nowadays, it is imperative that whoever communicates with the customer should have a full grasp of the issues facing all interaction with the customer and developments in each functional area. It makes sense to re-engineer the company around customer-facing processes. This requires all support activity to be reviewed, analysed and redesigned to meet the needs of the most important person of all – the customer. Although 'customer-facing processes' are targeted to be 100% effective, turning from a traditional to a re-engineered customer focus is one of the most difficult issues for any business. Many efforts failed because no attempt was made to develop a culture to support the re-engineering.

The careers of many managers have, in the past, been dependent upon their rise through functional hierarchies. Progression has usually been dependent on generating greater expertise and knowledge than your colleagues within the same functional area, rather than broadening the scope of experience cross-functionally and between organisation units.

Few accolades are bestowed on managers who willingly risk their continued progression through a function by moving sideways to gain cross-functional experience. An understanding of the whole process across departments, leading to understanding and operating the business from a different perspective, is very powerful in working towards improving service delivery. But how many companies really structure along these lines?

Building careers in re-engineered businesses is the challenge that HR specialists will have to confront. How do we reward people who sacrifice their specialism and seniority vertically by moving sideways for generalist experience? Many reward strategies continue to be geared towards the specialist rather than the generalist.

# Essentials for re-engineering for the customer

Re-engineering has got a bad name because people do not understand the enormity of the concept. Many confuse 'process flow mapping' as process re-engineering. The former is an O & M technique for foolproofing and revising processes; the latter is a major cultural change. You cannot have a re-engineering change without preceding it with a culture change. The empowered customer-focused culture needs to be in place before all who serve the customer come together to rethink the infrastructure that supports the customer.

Essentials for this work call for a thorough overview of the total customer contact. Customer service managers have to understand all interactions and be able to work with diverse groups. Moving a functional organisation to a team-driven business requires more than basic team-building skills: it requires that every customer is taken into account. Some customers will have different requirements. It could also arise that some of your customers are distant from you in terms of their commitment to culture change.

# Re-engineering requires a fit with corporate strategy.

Knowing where you are going, in a corporate sense, is essential to capitalise on any major change involving re-engineered processes. Sometimes this requires a fundamental rethink on corporate strategy. Because structure and systems always follow strategy and direction, it is useful to review strategy and plans for expansion and acquisition.

I have undertaken work with a variety of companies which have benefited from developing a strong vision of the directions they can pursue. Sharing information, using strategic planning models, making assumptions about the market place, reviewing core competitors and their strategies, reviewing substitutes for your product or service and barriers to entry amongst a host of other factors is critical. Recently, I worked with a top team to review their future. I was unhappy that assumptions being made about their future market were too general and open to interpretation. From this, I conducted a vulnerability analysis, looking at each of the geographies in which the company operated. Each was assessed according to potential growth and terms of trade, including their ability to pay for services. I also undertook an analysis of how the company was most vulnerable in each of its markets, devised preventative measures to override any vulnerability and built a business plan to reflect the investment required to generate a return. From this, I was able to prioritise which markets were most at risk; which would provide the best return; which were ready to be developed in the longer term; and those which were declining. This enabled me to resource teams that would supply and operate within these markets with the people best suited to achieve the objectives.

This exercise must take place in a culture where there is openness and full communication. This can only arise when those who manage the business locally are involved actively in decisions and debate, look at different perspectives, then make decisions about the business. Only when business plans are created can the business make an informed choice as to where priority service is to be focused.

Moving from the business planning stage, it is time to work through the optimum structure to support each of the markets. It will not work on traditional lines. It has to operate across the business, which requires a major exercise in ensuring that IT, systems, finance and customer service work seamlessly together with manufacturing and production. It is not the sort of event which can take place over a weekend. Neither do all re-engineering initiatives have an IT solution solely.

## To be effective, most re-engineering does not require a mega investment in IT

IT is not the only solution and for many companies it can actually stop them restructuring. It stops development because people identify a huge cost with IT development. My contention is that IT developments costs can be reduced by as much as 50% if customer-focused teams design and work through 80% of the planning prior to IT people taking over. What is more important is getting the processes, infrastructure and resulting relationships right, before moving on to devise IT solutions.

Working with people empowered to make decisions helps to get ideas down on paper. Serving the customer requires people to think outside the box. How can we speed up service delivery and delight the customer? One way is to simplify processes – not complicate them! Bureaucracy-busting is one way. Often processes are unfocused and customer-unfriendly because too many steps are geared to inspecting, checking, reviewing and controlling who does what.

**171**

Think of the alternative. What is stopping you being responsive and developing an innovative process geared and based upon foolproofing principles of error prevention, so that you don't have to over-check everything? You can still have an error-free process. Do not think that stages of over-control ensure that poor quality does not happen. All that over-inspection does is lengthen the process and illustrate a lack of trust, as well as take all personal responsibility out of the process.

If people can be brought together, they should look at the process as it operates – not as written down in a book. Walk through what actually happens. By doing this, you will see where problems arise. Then, using creative process mapping, (which is a million miles away from the O & M technique of flow charting), it is possible to create a sharp and responsive series of customer-focused processes. Remember, all of this could not exist without advanced team skills and action plans for implementation which reflect how people are going to work on projects in the future.

## Building a customer-focused culture

When driving any customer excellence process there is a requirement to focus on the internal supply chain – that intricate net of relationships which require people to work closely together. Here, as part of the re-engineering effort, key result areas need to be addressed, and reviewed, to identify non-conformances. Supply chain workshops can then be organised to ensure that service levels between internal suppliers and customers flow with ease and are error-free. Devoting time to team working is critical before engaging in external customer service. And although the external customer is more important than the internal, it is vital to ensure that everyone in-house is rowing in the same direction before going outside and dealing with customer facing real issues. The alternative is taking real problems and trying to get a solution based on functional lines. The solution will not fit the problem.

Part of this process is ensuring that the business needs to structure for change.

## Structure for change

In the last chapter we discussed the importance of reviewing layers and ensuring that form followed strategy.

**'Layers in an organisation are like wearing layers of sweaters. They isolate you from reality — they protect you from the cold. It's only when you take off the layers that you understand how cold it is. It's the same with layers of management. They isolate you from reality and what customers think.'**

Although this issue has been dealt with, it is so important that the company is perceived as being responsive to customer needs. It is like turning the organisational chart upside down. The people who are customer facing, sometimes the more junior team members, have more impact on customer service than more senior colleagues who never meet the customer. Some of your more junior staff probably liaise more effectively with the customer than the senior team.

People in order entry, finance and distribution all need advanced training in customer focus, which far outweighs 'smile training.' Smile training is best summed up as dealing with symptoms rather than the cause of customer disservice. Many companies have embarked upon expensive customer service programmes to find they were doing no more than providing staff with inter-personal skills to deal with customer complaints — not actually adding value to the customer at all.

Full customer service training can take place only after you have established what is important for each customer. Their perception of their needs can differ markedly from yours; it is best to test for understanding. Part of this process may mean getting your staff to spend time with your customers, finding out what it is like to receive service from your business. But generally this involves either conducting focus groups or using instruments to assess customer service levels.

Focus groups can be extremely powerful but must be conducted in a protected environment — for your business. You don't want one customer shouting what lousy service you provide in front of others who think you do a good job. For this reason, questionnaires and focused one-on-one telephone interviews can also be powerful. We use Mystery Shopping as a tool where the business has a number of retail outlets or branch offices, where service levels can be measured to assess how well we are dealing with the final consumer of goods or service.

To find out what it is really like to receive their service, the public sector and large service bureaucracies need to commit more to rigorous customer reviews and Mystery Shopping.

## What's important in customer service

An empowering culture of cross-functional working needs to exist prior to going out to the market to exclaim how good your service really is. This means having a programme of continuous improvement firmly in place so that, when there is a problem, there is an established way of dealing with it.

## Vision

As previously stated, if you don't have a vision of where the business is going, and how it's going to get there, how can your staff focus energy and talents to achieve it? When looking at the vision, and involving others in the process, it is important to review the quality and the effectiveness of corporate exhortations about service quality. When doing this, focus equally on internal and external customers/suppliers to ensure the message is clearly presented and received 'in-house'.

In creating a vision, you may want to think through what your business will look like in the future and whether you would describe it as an animal, film, meal, sport, machine or car. This is the impression that you want to create. If some people see the organisation as a 'dinosaur' and you see it as a 'lion', there's room for changing perceptions. This should be a fun event, one in which people really can contribute useful ideas.

## Listen and act on customers' views

The culture has to demonstrate that you really are listening to the customer, not just responding to what you think you can hear. This means welcoming customer complaints as opportunities for service improvement. Complaints are the best way of ensuring you do something about a problem. Customer statistics claim that, in instances when people feel they have received less than they expected, only about 20% of those aggrieved actually complain to the service provider. So, there are 80% of opportunities for improvement you cannot rectify because you are ignorant of them. To make matters worse, these 80% who feel aggrieved will, on average, tell at least six to eight people about their negative experience. So the negative cycle spreads and your poor service is communicated far and wide.

Create an internal system geared to improving performance and tie it in with an incentive scheme focused entirely on implementing best practice.

## Identify role models and benchmark

Assess your industry and look at how others deliver customer service. Focus upon breaking down service delivery into discrete chunks and look at best practices. From this, you can assess where you are in comparison to other service providers and assess where you are most vulnerable. You may ask yourselves 'What's the worst thing our competitors could do to us?' Take action to make sure this never happens.

From benchmarking where you are in your industry, it is advisable to start assessing where you fit in terms of non-industry examples who are classed as excellent.

## Develop everyone to remove all barriers to adding value

This major training event focuses on continuous improvement and requires a challenging attitude from staff at all levels. Cross-functional teams looking at process improvement, and the development of techniques to equip those who liaise most frequently with the customer to be able to improve performance. This must be a priority. Tailoring training using best inter-personal skills techniques and problem solving approaches, as appropriate, should become the norm.

Customer service teams can be formed to examine how to instil the positive response of customer delight and understand what causes irritation, annoyance, and compensation-seeking behaviour of those aggrieved with the service provided.

Beyond this, it is critical to have HR strategies geared towards creating 'champions of customer service' and attracting the best people into key positions.

## Summary and bullet points

The thin veneer and surface depth with which some organisations deal with their customers will have horrendous consequences for many businesses in the next few years. Large bureaucracies, both public and private, need to review how they deal with their customers. As we move into the 21st century, it will become increasingly obvious that people have more choice about those with whom they transact business.

Organisations which fail to re-engineer their customer service focus, and follow through with a rigorous infrastructure, are in for a shock.

- Consider who are the core constituents in the customer-focused strategy. Your customers are served by your staff; and your customer relations are very much a reflection of employee relations in the business.

- Organisations need to be committed to retaining their customers. It costs five times as much to recruit a new customer — how much easier to service the existing customer and plunder from your competitors those who are dis-satisfied.

- The only acceptable quality level is 100%

- The customer covers all costs of failure.

- Remember the 'iceberg of ignorance'. How much don't you know about the level of customer failure in your business?

- Re-engineer all processes to become customer-focused.

- Customer focus should be speedy, error-free and seamless when received by your customer.

- Re-engineered processes need to be supported by innovative incentive and development strategies.

- Re-engineering requires a major culture change to support it.

- Moving from a functionally-driven, to a process-driven, team-driven, culture is the biggest problem facing re-engineering.

- Customer service managers have to control, and understand, all interactions from supplier to customers and ensure all processes have closed loops.

- Re-engineering must have a firm fit with corporate strategy.

- In 90% of cases, re-engineering requires a major rethink in corporate strategy.

- Corporate strategy is a highly interactive process which requires input from those local to the market, together with a strategic overview.

- A good corporate strategy requires significant commitment to markets, product portfolio, maturity, risk, vulnerability analysis and testing for understanding. It cannot be completed over a weekend.

- Most re-engineering does not require a mega investment in IT.

- Build a customer-focused culture from the inside out.

- Structure for change – first!

- Create a firm, tangible, focused, easy to understand and exciting vision.

- Listen and respond to customer complaints.

- Take a complaint as an opportunity to improve performance.

- Identify role models and benchmark your progress.

- Only align with, and emulate, the best.

# Chapter 14:

# Speed of Change – you're fast or you're dead

In the new century 'speed of implementing change' will be the key differentiator separating companies which succeed from those which fail. When introducing changes, many senior officers fail to realise that time is not on their side. In order to outperform, outmanoeuvre and outpace competitors, organisations need to adopt a 'fleet of foot' approach to installing a quick and effective method for implementing key changes. This final chapter examines, and suggests methods to overcome, the barriers to speed of implementation.

## Let's get real – change is here to stay

The process of change is here to stay. Over 25 years ago, Alvin Toffler, expounding the process in his book, *Future Shock*, expressed the view that the rate of change impacting upon society, organisations and people was constantly accelerating. He predicted how we should cope with change and implied there would be many casualties if the process was ignored.

So, many years later, one would imagine that this warning, predicting a dire need to master the process of change, would be instilled in everyone involved in the dynamic world of business and commerce. Sadly, this is not the case. Many organisations have failed to equip themselves with staff and managers who can understand and, positively manage the process.

Change, a process of adaptation, can be learned and controlled, although many seem to fear it.

I appreciate that changes which impact upon 'business as usual' are often inconvenient, and could come at a better time. But that is what managing resources is all about – coping with ambiguity and implementing in times of increasing complexity and uncertainty. Change is successful only when 100% implementation is ensured. You may wish to consider the changes which have affected your enterprise, to think through those that were successfully implemented and those that were not.

## Why don't we assess the success rate of change?

We are aware that very many change or re-engineering initiatives associated with changing corporate culture falter at the first hurdle and have to be rejuvenated. Assess your own organisation's attempts to bring about re-engineering of processes across functions, the implementation of MRP or JIT. More importantly, consider the future. For those in the public sector, Health Trusts and the like, consider the focus on the customer, the implementation of CCT and other initiatives.

Many seem to believe that all the changes which impact upon organisations should queue up, like customers, outside the building in an orderly manner, patiently waiting for the last change to be conveniently implemented by the management team before another is attended to. The peculiar Anglo Saxon habit of expecting things to happen in order, when we live in a dynamic world, still surprises me when we have seen significant changes in recent years.

**'The Berlin Wall may come down but in the average organisation we still have to wait until the end of the summer holidays before we can implement anything!'**

Working with an organisation which I will not name, I have been collecting excuses from a small group of senior and middle managers who constantly find reasons not to implement changes. After listening to why something could not be done, I carefully catalogued some of the world changes which have taken place in the 90s. We talked through the fall of the Berlin Wall, the brave and successful attempts of the West Germans to integrate with the East through massive investment. Likewise, the collapse of the USSR and the self-determination of the Soviet and Baltic states has caused major global friction. Similarly, the changes in China, the collapse of communism, the Gulf

War, the threat to world peace have all created some uncertainty. The explosion in consumer power of the Far East as the next customer revolution, with the West as potential suppliers (and also losers if we don't live up to expectations) has all meant that we have had to think and operate in a global rather than local market place.

## Let's take perspective

What these global changes have in common is that, in scope and scale, they were largely unpredicted. Yet many people have controlled these forces in some form or shape. The use of these global analogies are examples to help us take perspective of our problems and take charge. If it is possible to manage conflict and complexity on a grand scale, as previously indicated, introducing change into a fairly steady state system which employs hundreds or thousands of people is manageable.

## Let's be glo-cal, not global or local

The coming together of 'global and local' creates a marketplace which we can call 'glocal' — requiring a global vision while responding to local needs faster than our competitors.

## Change is not a logical process

This does not mean the process can't be controlled with patience, effort and work. Many hold the belief that the change process should be a rational process. Experience tells us that change is often a random process which outwits the predictions of rational, intelligent and orderly people. Econometric models of the economy, international currency movements and increased house prices should be seen for what they are — an attempt to model or regulate the world, but not a true reflection of what happens in the world.

The problem with models of change is that, as soon as they are developed and tested, they are out of date. We live in a dynamic world and other variables of which we were unaware have impinged and carefully destroyed all the good work that the theorists have done. So avoid the belief that change falls into steps or categories and perceive change as an incremental process of flow.

## Distrust static models of change

Throw away the texts that outline the change process comprising a set or number of stages which have be carefully and sequentially worked through before change is effectively implemented. Change is an incremental process. In other words, the steps we take today are influenced by people, other actors in the dynamic flow of things. Their actions or inactions will impact upon the development of the process. We also have to appreciate the change process by where you and others stand when viewing implementation. For instance, it is always easier to manage change if you have been ordained to drive it. Those who drive a business should have the handle on change. The next level of management may have a different view of change. Supervisors and staff have a different interpretation because they have not yet taken ownership of it. Your position on the transition curve will determine how you react and how you behave. The responsibility of managers is to get all key people in the process to take ownership of change.

## Our focus should be on the theory of action

There is no point believing that the changes which affect us will wait in an orderly fashion until we are ready to deal with them. We have to respond with action. We have to develop an approach based on taking purposeful action. If prepared, managers or staff have the resources to deal with most changes. By adopting a methodology of action which is driven by discipline (project management), the fear of change will not exist. The old phrase 'anticipation is worse than the experience itself' could not be more true. We need to equip staff to move out of familiar comfort zones to work on new challenges.

## Why don't managers respond quickly enough?

The reason managers don't respond quickly enough is mostly to do with attitude, an issue which can be redressed through training. By providing additional training focused upon 'reframing the implications of change', it is almost certain they will be able to handle the process successfully.

Above all, as in any development work, managers need to practise skills in order to become proficient. Training and development initiatives need to move away from the technical focus of training and knowing towards doing and implementing. Training which focuses upon 'doing' and 'practising new behaviours' is critical if we hope to develop an almost unconscious competence in the new skills. I call it a competence at the unconscious level because it becomes second nature and automatic, as automatic as using a keyboard or driving a car.

## A few words on unconscious competence.

Managers need to be trained to cope with change, deal with complexity and take thoughtful risks. Development of competence should focus upon instilling core skills and competencies. Real core competence is driving the process of change through facilitation.

## Flow rather than control

Too many staff concentrate on trying to 'control' the variables in change rather than letting the process flow and making changes as they arise. Old style managers have yet to learn that trying to control variables does not lead to implementation – it breeds a 'one best way' approach.

Change, by its very nature, relies on how people adapt. Often the models we create leave out the most unpredictable part of the change, the reactions and behaviours of others. For this reason, it is critical to develop flexibility and flow in implementation. There are more than one, two or three ways to improve things – it just depends on where the ownership for change is positioned and who is committed to the process. Reject the 'one best way' approach and develop flexibility.

## Speed is critical as the next key differentiator

Some senior staff fail to recognise that 'speed is the essence' However, the challenge for changes in management style and focus has fallen to a great extent upon deaf ears. We still hear the faint cry from the dinosaurs that we should "slow down in order to consolidate." This is impossible. The challenge for the late 90s and beyond is to become obsessively focused on responsiveness and adapt faster to the opportunities and threats that await us. Make no mistake, the key is to be even more responsive with our customers. Speed will be the differentiator in winning or losing business.

To illustrate the point, let us concentrate on a case study where speed is the differentiator in the market.

Working regularly in the financial services industry, I recognise that the products in the same sector are roughly the same, no matter who is the provider. Interest rates, terms and conditions, lease agreements and residual values are broadly similar. However, what is increasingly more important to the customer than features of the product, is speed of response. One of my long-standing clients prides itself on being able to respond to the demands of business clients in minutes, rather than days, the performance standard of its competitors. The company in question provides point of sale finance to the motor industry. Those who manage the business recognised a long time ago that customers do not want to wait days to see if a finance company will underwrite the transaction. Customers need to know immediately. When competitors take too long to reach decisions, they lose market share.

The leading edge company, GE Capital, understands that delighting the customer, i.e. responding in minutes, is what creates a stable future and market. Competitors still think that quality alone is sufficient and pride themselves on the quality of underwriting they provide. In honesty, what separates the high performer from the 'also ran' is quality, coupled with speed of response. This is the new formula for success. Deliver error-free and faster service than your competitors and you win the business.

Regarding change in the public and private sector, the real problem when discussing change is that many managers believe the process relates only to the private sector, although change has never been faster in any sector. Change is speeding up and engulfing many organisations. The reason they are being engulfed is that managers choose not to cope with the speed required to deal with complex changes.

There are several reasons why change, often perceived as a barrier to progress, is not taken seriously. If these barriers are not shattered, we will never be able to achieve our potential. Let's look at a successful change initiative where speed was paramount:

*Commitment to change: the housing department*

*After working with a housing department within a district council in Scotland, I was delighted to find that, even though reorganisation of the District structure was imminent, the top team was committed to culture change. Their commitment lay in training their top 30 managers in the process. The advantage of this approach was that top managers, in turn, could facilitate change. This was far more important than training managers how to use packaged training. From this effort, ten teams of three managers cascaded the process down through their respective departments. They are currently involved in action planning and working on problem-solving. They willingly committed to the process knowing that, by training their staff to process change, they had equipped themselves with the most important tool for change – creation of a management group which understood, practised and facilitated change.*

## What about change in the last 25 years?

If by magic, we could use a Time Machine to travel back into the industrial past, we would come across industries which appeared to be thriving. In the mid-sixties we would see a thriving motorcycle and car industry, as well as shipbuilding, iron and steel, transportation, and a strong, home produced and owned, consumer durable market. The late 60s and early 70s would present us with an electronic promise for the future, with thriving companies providing all sorts of components for the IT/IS revolution. Coming right along the time line, what happened to these businesses? And what of tomorrow?

*Now let's explore an initiative in financial services: Mortgage Express*

## *Mortgage Express, winner of the British Quality Award 1996: A Real Change Maker*

*(Excerpts from an article by Philip Atkinson and Peter Taylor, HR and Quality Manager, Mortgage Express)*

*This case study outlines the radical steps taken by the top team of Mortgage Express to rapidly introduce culture change. The successful implementation of the change was determined by the leadership, cohesiveness, tenacity and energy of the directors driving the process. Values were outlined as key drivers but managerial or leadership behaviour was also a strong leverage point. Involvement of people was central to things actually happening.*

*After the collapse of the housing market, the new management team purpose for Mortgage Express in 1991 was simple – exit from new business and initiate a transfer back to the parent company, TSB. Within two years, they had initiated a measurable improvement in culture through Total Quality and been shortlisted to four from a list of 200 applications for the 1995 British Quality Award.*

*In 1994, Mortgage Express was dangerously close to shutting its doors with a potential loss of all 350 jobs. This was in response to house prices falling rapidly in the early 90s, leaving many home owners with negative equity.*

### *Withdrawal from the market*
*The effect on corporate morale was devastating, with many employees expressing anxiety over possible job losses.*

- *How did the board react?*

- *How could they manage the transfer while maintaining superior customer service?*

- *What action should they take to stop the movement of high calibre staff to other businesses?*

- *What strategy could the top team create to ensure that Mortgage Express (MX) retained a loyal, committed and motivated workforce?*

*With the threat of falling motivation, the top team had to plan and implement a strategy which would ensure staff were retained. This was key if the company was to service 30,000 customers effectively.*

*The top team: becoming self critical*
*Understanding that change starts with self was an important factor in driving the MX team to turn their company around. They placed more emphasis on building on the performance-driven culture of the business.*

*Assumptions behind the strategy*
*The MX concept is known as 'employability'. The organisational responsibilities are to:*

- *Ensure a sense of challenge and achievement.*
- *Maximise opportunities for an individual team to bring about improvement.*
- *Enable*
- *Facilitate*
- *Recognise and ensure continuous development.*

- *Individual responsibilities are to take charge, seek opportunities, be flexible, continually learn and have fun.*

*With transfer focused on the last quarter of 94 or first quarter 95, the top team took the following actions:*

*All staff were to be involved eventually in the process – with, first, behaviours being discussed and developed through the direct reports to the top team. Special provision was made to ensure that this was cascaded within the business. Every member of staff attended a launch briefing followed by two interactive workshops to identify issues. Written information on mission and values was sent to every member of staff.*

*Direct reports to the top team underwent significant training, concentrating on change management, leadership and sustaining a positive culture.*

*Quality improvement and the UK Quality Award.*
*One evening, after working through the key issues, the top team expressed their commitment to quality improvement for this award, with less than a year before submission of the proposal. Having used the UK / European Quality model approach over a three year period, all at senior levels understood the commitment needed to produce a 'quality' application. A project team, volunteers from across the business, was formed, with over 80 people contributing, often in their own time, so that the 75-page application document could be completed. The project, lasting six months, was a great success. So much so that Mortgage Express had a number of requests from other companies to buy their application document. A unique feature was the cover design, a photograph of all staff; and every employee received a copy of the application.*

*Many developed and attended formalised programmes, while others sought opportunities in open learning. Staff felt free to choose their learning outcomes and be responsible for mastering that learning. This created a passionate learning environment in which some staff pursued MBAs and professional qualifications, while others sampled the delights of practical skills.*

*There has been a substantial boost to already-high morale. All the investment in development has paid off and all staff feel they made personal commitment and effort in helping to turn the business around. This commitment is reflected in phenomenal levels of very high staff satisfaction: over 75%, on average, in the last three years (culture survey results).*

*Since February 1995, the company has maintained its commitment to development of staff and formed a strong platform upon which to consolidate human resource initiatives.*

*Creating facilitators for change: neuro linguistics*
*Mortgage Express is keenly aware that the quality of its managers determines the quality of the business. In particular, the company believes it should maintain its own army of internal change agents, rather than rely solely on external consultancies.*

*The single most important desirable characteristic of the MX manager for the future goes far beyond his or her technical ability; it resides in an ability to manage the process of change. Managers are attending advanced programmes on inter-personal influence and facilitation. Success now, and in the future, is based on the ability to persuade and influence others to achieve results, thereby rejecting a 'control' culture.*

*The content of such programmes goes far beyond models of change and techniques of problem-solving and decision-making. The process of change can be understood only when we understand how people communicate, influence and work together. Special emphasis is given to neuro linguistics and working with others to develop joint outcomes.*

*Culture change: staff opinion questionnaire*

*Traditionally a process owned by the HR Director and his staff, a regular staff survey is now driven and developed through an inter-disciplinary improvement team, which has taken responsibility to regularly benchmark company culture. Managers have a precise measurement tool for assessing the culture within their own function; and gain additional insight on how they interact with key internal customers and suppliers.*

*Mortgage Express formally went back into the mortgage-lending market in September 1995, again with a team of staff working incredibly long hours in order to make a success of the venture. As a result new niche markets have been identified and innovative products have been developed.*

*Entering the UK Quality award programme provided a very positive motivational focus for the business; a key criterion was how to further improve the business. With more than 200 applications, MX was short-listed to the final four in 1995. Jubilant staff began working enthusiastically on their 1996 submission.*

---

*Mortgage Express wins 1997 British Quality Award*

*The MX team worked extremely hard, again hoping to do well. They won the award – an incredible achievement in such a short time, one which will guide them forward.*

*Mortgage Express acquired by Bradford & Bingley*

*In the summer of 1997, Mortgage Express was purchased by Bradford & Bingley, into whose network they would fit as a niche business. Going back two or three years, how many people in the industry held out any hope for Mortgage Express? But through dedication of the workforce, they were able to build a new culture. Not many organisations will commit to this degree of change; and too many don't think they CAN change.*

*Review*

*A final point. Ask yourself how many companies with closure looming would move beyond a 'quick fix' mentality to develop a new culture and be short-listed for the BQA?  And for the cynics: what effect did working with the soft side of culture have on the bottom line?  The facts are:*

- *Turning a £67 million loss in 1992 to a £38 million profit in 1994.*
- *Improving customer satisfaction by over 28% and significantly improving staff satisfaction by 75%.*
- *The top team turned the business around by building a new culture. They are open for business again.*

---

If we could use the same time machine to travel 20 years into the future, will we still see the giants in banking, finance and insurance? Would we witness businesses structured and focused entirely on customer responsiveness? Will we see flat organisations, focused on partnering with clients with service delivered by empowered staff working across boundaries? If we don't see this vision, we have a major problem: we have not learned from our mistakes.

## Commit to change now.

How we have confronted change in the past is a testimony to today's business world. Whether we are captains of industry, supervisors or junior staff, we need to develop an optimistic view of change. If we are not to lose our niche businesses, we need to take this issue seriously. To achieve a solid future we need to do several things:

## Ten steps towards speedy effective implementation

### 1. Top team commitment towards the learning organisation

The learning organisation is focused on surveying best practices in other industries, markets and sectors, choosing to implement processes which are most appropriate, and doing it quickly.

This requires critically assessing organisational practices and encouraging staff to go outside their comfort zone to look at what others are doing in the same industry; then looking at best practice outside it. By encouraging this challenging and critical attitude, organisations can grow a healthy 'benchmarking' culture where customer responsiveness and continuous improvement become the key goals of the business.

An organisation I work with runs staff action teams involved in re-engineering a process away from the traditional 'functional' to a speedier 'customer focus'. All key staff concerned with working the process are employed off-site until a 'customer-focused' solution is found. (Often customers are involved in the process). There are no time constraints. Participants in the process may work away from home for three or four days but the investment pays dividends. Resources are deployed to facilitate progress. Preventing problems and working on new solutions is valued highly. Once the solution has been worked out and agreed, the team has 48 hours to implement the solution on site. Most activity in implementing the solution is communicating to and winning the support of, other staff to create the right infrastructure in which the new process will develop. Some of the expensive re-engineering methodologies are rejected in favour of this quicker approach. It is more effective because owners work on the new process; the end result must be customer delight and improved customer responsiveness.

## 2. Indecision breeds risk aversion

Senior staff sometimes have difficulties when thinking through options they should take when reappraising business culture, infrastructure and processes. Decisions will be delayed because of intangibles. For instance, how can the new customer service team run on a self-managed basis? Can we afford to let our branch network go so quickly when sales people are working from home?

Decisions like these are based upon a lack of faith in the people. By giving more control, staff take more responsibility for the process – they become process owners rather than process operators. The culture of control is replaced by one of trust. This does not come about overnight and is based upon developing staff over time. This only comes about through an informal appraisal process geared to developing people to fulfil the role you see for them, and designing training accordingly. Adopting this approach pays big dividends and sends to staff the message that personal potential is is being stretched.

Thoughtful 'stretching' breaks staff away from their comfort zones and encourages them to take thoughtful risks based on looking at new, and better, ways to deliver customer service. Most organisations could benefit from developing this component in their culture. This alone helps to move towards empowerment and growth.

## 3. Customers want responsiveness

Unless you have spent the last five years in Siberia, you will be aware that customers crave responsiveness. Many senior officers are still unaware of the customer revolution. Working with a big, US-owned, business I was not surprised to see a major contract for supply of financial services (worth millions of £s) transferred to another provider. The reason? The original provider was too slow. Its internal processes were too bureaucratic, time-consuming and not focused on customer needs.

We are constantly amazed to find organisations less than speedy with internal and external customers. I have always maintained if we can't get the act right with the internal customer, we are probably doing a worse job with the external customer. Companies need to use 'customer friendly' methods to re-engineer processes towards the customer. Such processes are focused more upon the infrastructure of the business, and doing business with itself, than working on ways to do more business with existing external customers.

## 4. Empowerment starts by letting go

Empowerment, like re-engineering, is one of today's most misunderstood words. Too many perceive it as relaxed management control. Too many believe it is delegation dressed up in fancy plumage. Let us be specific. Empowerment has nothing to do with outlining what people can and cannot do – it has nothing to do with increasing, policing and enforcing limits.

Empowerment starts when the manager takes a risk, and stretches him or herself to 'let go' with staff. This means trusting the ability of staff to take ownership. It also means supporting staff if things do not go well – living the culture of trust, not control.

One test to measure the degree to which empowerment is real and living is illustrated below. When staff start suggesting, and volunteering, for changes they will instigate themselves, empowerment can be said to be starting to flourish.

Staff will challenge their manager to look at things differently. Empowerment is a clear element of the culture when, and only when, the manager encourages a 360 degree appraisal of his/ her performance, by boss, colleagues and staff.

Taken in this context, empowerment is mutual trust. And when you have empowerment, you don't need people managing. The manager becomes coach, facilitator and leader and acquires new skills to cope with his or her new role.

## 5. Resistance to change

I always have difficulty when people tell me they love change. The difficulty is that, when people tell me this, they are usually managing the process. Being on the receiving end of an edict can create a different impression, so I introduce an important, but simple rule: what would it be like to receive this message about the change from you?

Setting managers to appreciate that the message is what is received, not what is sent, is critical. If they look at the process of change, and what people will 'receive' from their messages, they tend to adopt a different process and new ways to relay the message they are communicating.

For instance, when I worked with a Health Trust, the then chief executive realised that traditional briefing was not working. In some areas, it was happening; in others, notes were pinned to notice boards and no discussion took place; and in a few areas there was two-way communication. To this CEO the issue was so important that he decided to brief his top 60 people (four groups) himself on key issues facing the Trust. He devoted one day to taking each of the four groups of his most senior staff, including several directors, through the process. This was a good way to ensure that messages, in times of change, were well communicated. The 60 attending, usually once a fortnight, clearly understood the message because it was delivered coherently and consistently. They, in turn, repeated the process down through the structure.

Generalising from this example I have yet to see, or hear of, an occasion when senior staff over-communicate. Bearing this in mind, does it suggest that those in managerial positions should portray superior interpersonal and communication skills?

## 6. Manage transitions

We can see, feel and hear a series of processes in every change initiative: shock, denial, unlearning, relearning and integration. Depending upon which part of the curve you occupy your response will differ. Recognising where 'you are' determines what you see, hear and feel about the change.

Simply by identifying the processes you are experiencing will determine your commitment to the change. If you are in denial, nothing that I or others will say will move you from that emotional state. However, if I anticipate you will go through the process of shock when an announcement is made, I can readdress my message to deal with the key issues which arise – for example, reality testing. So, for instance, I could take preventative action to ensure all issues were dealt with at each of these stages. This approach encourages managers to explore the importance of communication. It must be remembered that if managers have superior communication skills, and influence by persuasion rather than control, there would be little resistance to change. There is no such thing as intransigent staff, just inflexible communicators.

## 7. Train in interpersonal skills and NLP

Superior communication skills associated with Neuro Linguistic Programming (NLP) will be a radical growth area in the next ten to 20 years. The relatively new science, based on modelling excellence in communication, is barely 20 years old and evolving all the time. Before we try to figure out how to communicate and influence others, we have to learn first how we communicate with ourselves in terms of personal motivation and drive. This means exploring our personal beliefs and values and whether we view the world in a pessimistic or optimistic way.

As a Trainer of NLP, I use the techniques to help people with personal changes, moving them away from self-limiting beliefs ("I'll never be able to do that") towards wanting to improve performance and, thus, personal development.

We achieve results through people. So it should come as no surprise that equipping people with these skills considerably improves their ability to influence others to achieve stretching targets and work more effectively as team members.

## 8. Invest in your people

There is probably no danger of an organisation over-training staff to work on the process of change. Bearing this in mind, it is critical to work out the key skills which you need to manage your business not just now, but in five or ten years' time. Forward-thinking businesses identify, and train their staff quickly, in core competencies.

I believe core competencies fall in the area of communication and change management. Encouraging managers to replace 'control' with 'trust' does not happen without an injection of enthusiasm and skill. Skill is the operative word because it implies that practise is vitally important. As we have each adopted skills to drive a car, speak foreign languages or play an instrument, we have gone through the process of over-learning. In other words, our learning has become an unconscious process – we don't have to consciously think of every movement, word or note in order to demonstrate our competence. This is the same standard we need to develop with what I call the 'meta' skills of communication and change management. We should practise until we are an expert. Then we don't even have to think about them – because they are mastered.

## 9. Deal with cultural and leadership issues

I have never liked the word manager because it conjures up measurement, control and restriction. Leadership and coaching conjure up a climate of trust and team work. Once the decision is made to change from one culture to another, go for it. Focus upon the advantages of having a group of committed, enthusiastic staff able to practise their skills to improve service.

We need to recognise that culture exists in some organisations 98% by default and accident rather than by design. But this can be turned around by the top team if there is commitment to change. The most powerful action in influencing cultural change is 'to what leaders pay most attention.' Research has highlighted that this is the most significant factor in changing a culture. Without Leadership, there is no change.

Many have over-estimated the time it takes to change a culture. It does not take two, four or six years. It takes as long as you want it to take.

## 10. Create a team of internal facilitators – line managers

Successful organisations have a trained team of line managers who can facilitate change on many levels. It doesn't matter if change is involved with TQ, culture, MRP, JIT, re-engineering, re-structuring, downsizing, system integration. The process of change is the same because we can only change through people and working with teams. Once an organisation is equipped with an internal capability to manage the process, reliance on external sources diminishes.

A further advantage is that this leads to significant personal development of staff at senior level; there will be a noticeable improvement in general management of resources and the business. The final point is that change should always reside in the line, not with human resources. HR people can be extremely useful advisors but lasting change takes place only when front liners see their direct line manager as a coach, leading and facilitating the process of change.

## Summary and bullet points

Business is conducted on a global basis. What happens in one part of the world can have a massive impact upon business in our own area of expertise. With the speedy flow of information available to help us make business decisions, we recognise that now, more than ever before, we have to develop a planned approach to strategic planning and crisis prevention. Because our focus is on global efforts, we have to ensure that operational issues are dealt with at the key interface by those best suited to do it. We have to transfer responsibility to those who own the process – in other words those who work it – not those who manage it. This is true empowerment.

- Organisations which are going to succeed are learning organisations. Those that manage them will hold a strong value on scanning and surveying the environment, benchmarking best practices within their own industry and others and implementing these practices faster than their competitors.

- Implementation is the key to success. Speedy implementation is the key to maintaining, consolidating and creating market share.

**197**

• Speed of implementation is exciting and, when matched with quality of service, is unbeatable. We need to appreciate that the marketplace is becoming more and more complex. As each day passes, we are better or worse than our competitors. If we are standing still it, probably means that others are passing us by. And that implies we are going backwards.

• The key factor that will determine a secure future is speedily responding to what the customer and the market wants, and when and how it wants it. This has to be delivered faster than your competitors. It can be achieved by equipping yourself with managers and staff who have mastered, and led the processes of change.

# APPENDIX

## Video training packages

### TQ and Culture Change Series

**A Tool for Changing Behaviour: The Johari Window**. 15 minutes. Philip Atkinson explains that any change requires managers to become more critical of their own behaviour and the impact that this has on those they manage. He describes the Johari Model of examining behaviour from the perspective of those things which are known to others and to oneself. A great video package for starting the process of personal change and one which focuses in-depth on the process.
**£230.00 + VAT**

**Building Lasting Customer Relationships.** Critical for any organisation is the way we deal with and focus on our customers. This 30-minute video concentrates upon the importance of encouraging customer complaints and examines the poor statistics associated with customer retention. The average service business will lose 80% of its customer base every five years. This video examines the importance of customer care with both the external and the internal customer.
**£385.00 + VAT.**

**Change management: Listening Skills.** 15 minutes. Change is achieved only when others can be influenced by those who lead. The requirement for developing effective listening skills is outlined. The video illustrates the key problems associated with poor listening and suggests actions which managers can take to improve personal performance.
**£230.00 + VAT.**

**Costing Quality.** 30 minutes. Here Philip Atkinson explains the major components of the Cost of Quality and highlights literally hundreds of examples of Rework. The philosophy which underpins the investment in Prevention to eliminate Rework is well explained by highlighting the importance of working across functional boundaries and getting things right in the planning process.
**£385.00 + VAT.**

**Creating Culture Change.** A 45-minute video filmed in front of a live audience and focusing upon the mainstay of culture and what it means. Corporate Culture is explored and Leadership as a foundation for effective change is highlighted. Applicable in a variety of organizational contexts.
**£250.00 + VAT.**

**Problem-Solving and Empowerment.** 20 minutes. This features a facilitator within GE Capital running a Work-out session for staff from different functions. Brainstorming and problem-solving are displayed within the group. A focused discussion on Empowerment provides an enthusiastic spur for organizations keen to pursue TQ.
**£250.00 + VAT.**

**Simple Models for Personal Change.** An extremely powerful video to be used when running a programme focusing on personal change. This would be ideal for examining behaviour in a team, leading and motivating, coaching and appraising others. Philip draws on two models for personal change - the Conscious Competence model and the Johari Window. This 15-minute video is extremely effective at getting people to adopt a more self-critical appraisal of the way their behaviour impacts upon others.
**£230.00 + VAT.**

**TQ: Leading the Process.** 35 minutes. This video focuses on the importance of Leadership in shaping corporate culture and draws upon several contemporary models of Leadership. Directors of GE Capital are interviewed and share their strong views on the importance of challenging and stretching staff.
**£385.00 + VAT**

**TQ: Steps to Implementation.** This is the most recent video on the pitfalls of introducing TQ and Culture Change. During this 30-minute video Philip Atkinson outlines the key issues which relate to unsuccessful implementation of change. He highlights why 80% plus initiatives fail and focuses upon a tangible method of assessing culture and talking through corporate strategy, leadership, values and people management.
**£285.00 + VAT**

*To order any of these videos, please contact: Transformations UK Ltd., 11 Alva Street, Edinburgh, EH2 4PH, tel: 0131 346 1276/226 4519, fax: 0131 346 1618, email: phil@transform.win-uk.net, quoting BTB. Why not visit our web site: http://www.lookhere.co.uk/transform/*

# Index